Revolutionary STATEN ISLAND

Revolutionary STATEN ISLAND

From Colonial Calamities to Reluctant Rebels

Joe Borelli

THE History PRESS

Published by The History Press
Charleston, SC
www.historypress.com

Front cover: Jasper Cropsey's *Cortelyou Farm* gives a glimpse of what the South Shore looked like in early America. *Staten Island Historical Society.*

First published 2020

Manufactured in the United States

ISBN 9781467147620

Library of Congress Control Number: 2020938466

To my sons,
John and Joseph

CONTENTS

INTRODUCTION

Once upon a time there was an island of incomparable beauty called Aquahonga.

Nearly 125 years ago, as Richmond County stood on the precipice of its consolidation with the other four boroughs, an unknown author published a short article in the *New York Sun* titled "Aquahonga," which is believed to be the Native American name for Staten Island. In the article, he described how the scenic and tranquil island would surely be lost, eventually to become the "new Bowery of Greater New York." He ended with the line: "It will be a very many long years before a historian can tell a story beginning with the words: 'Once upon a time there was an island of incomparable beauty called Aquahonga.'"[1]

Today, his prophecy is realized, and like him, I hope this book helps paint a picture of what this county was before it joined in the experiment called the City of Greater New York. For centuries, it was independent and had a unique historical relevance in its own right. Although we have not yet become the Bowery, this is the story of an island of incomparable beauty when it was a unique part of America's colonial experience and war for liberty.

Most islanders take for granted that it was the borough's twentieth-century history that shaped its modern footing, and in large part they're right. Politicians of that era are responsible for giving Staten Island its current building stock and suburban feel. Postwar Staten Island grew as New York's population swelled, automobiles became household commodities, public construction projects were in full swing and middle-class flight to the suburbs was the norm.

That chapter of Staten Island's history is not the focus of this book, nor is it the island's role as a borough of New York City. We look further back to a time when New York City, and the United States itself, did not exist as it does now. Of course, a history of early Richmond could not ignore that it has always been inherently linked to the island of Manhattan. However, for the majority of the county's history, as far back as its earliest settlers, it existed as a separate entity with its own municipalities, subdivisions and partially autonomous government. In fact, some New York historians, like CUNY's George J. Lankevich, have even suggested that modern Staten Island's unique perspective of its place in New York City is a holdover from the Dutch patroon system, when settlers first felt that they suffered under the "alien customs" of colonial governments in Manhattan.[2]

Staten Island's history is worth remembering. It was one of the first places that European explorers set their eyes on in modern America. It saw some of the earliest contacts with native peoples in 1524. It is one of the oldest settled counties in the country. Its colonial history predates that of the British at Philadelphia and the French in Louisiana. It was populated by successive waves of immigration, beginning in the 1700s with the Dutch and French and continued unbroken to the twentieth century. It was the site of war, misery, progress, prosperity, failure, fear and dense forests.

The first chronicle of the borough's history was John Jay Clute's *Annals of Staten Island, From Its Discovery to the Present Time.* The author was a historian and genealogist and, like me, served in public office. He was a collector of antiquities and acquired, in his words, "a large amount of interesting materials relating to the history of Staten Island."[3] His purpose for writing was to preserve the legacy of the "old people" he had known throughout his life, especially those of the Revolutionary War generation, whose memories he hoped to record for posterity. Particularly, he focused on why political sentiments shifted from loyalism to the cause of liberty over the course of the war, especially after the "licentiousness and rapacity" of encamped British soldiers.[4]

Ten years later, another chronicle was published by Richard M. Bayles, titled *A History of Richmond County, (Staten Island) New York, from Its Discovery to the Present Time*, and in 1898, Ira K. Morris published *Morris's History of Staten Island, New York*. However, Charles Leng and William T. Davis completed the most comprehensive five-volume history of the county between 1929 and 1933. *Staten Island and Its People, A History, 1609–1929* details the borough's chronology and adds encyclopedic articles on prominent people, places and institutions. Leng and Davis are also noteworthy as founders of the Staten Island Institute of Arts and Sciences and the Staten Island Historical Society, both still in existence. There is a wildlife sanctuary in Travis and school in St. George bearing Davis's name, and Willowbrook is home to the Charles W. Leng Middle School.

It was through reading *Staten Island and Its People* that I became interested in the county's past. After receiving my bachelor's degree in history from Marist College, I took a part-time job at Casey Funeral Home on Slosson Avenue. One of my easier duties was to man the office late into the night and wait for inevitable phone calls from nursing homes or family members. In between those conversations were hours of quiet solitude as I struggled (often unsuccessfully) to stay awake. The Caseys had been in the business for generations, and luckily for me, they had the rare original prints of the book on a basement bookshelf. Had the iPhone been invented by 2004, I might have never turned the cover. Yet, one hundred pages or so in, I was hooked.

Now, as then, Staten Island deserves an examination of its history, not merely as a part of New York City but also on its own, as just about every scene of America's story has played out on our shores. Hopefully, this tale of how Staten Island came to be is as interesting and relevant to readers today as it was when Leng and Davis put pen to paper in 1929.

1
THE COLLISION OF CONTINENTS

As the sun rose on a calm spring day in April 1524, those living on the island of Aquahonga Monocknong began their morning business as any other. At that time of year, the women were at work using shell and wooden hoes to plant beans and corn, while the men hunted throughout the island's wooded hills and set fishing nets along the muddy river that kept it divided from the mainland.[5]

That morning, while peering through the dense trees of the high ridgeline that runs along the island's eastern shore, one of the natives must have noticed a sight never before seen and well beyond what could have ever been imagined. "Look!" he or she would have shouted in their Algonquian tongue to others in the community.

A boat, grander and more complex than any in their known world, grew larger among the waves as it slowly approached from the southeastern horizon. As it drew near, the natives may have originally mistaken it for a giant waterfowl or sea creature, but soon its vast white sails arrayed among its three masts might have resembled a thick fog amid trees. In all likelihood, the sheer size and intricacies of its wooden decks were larger than any man-made structure that had ever met their eyes.

The ship continued to draw closer to the coast before making an abrupt stop in the approach to the narrow strait of water separating the island of Aquahonga from its neighboring, larger island to the east. At that point, the natives had a clear line of sight. They were keenly aware that on board those wooden decks and among the masts, now laying at anchor in the bay

In 1524, Giovanni da Verrazano (1485–1528) became the first European to pass through the Narrows separating Staten Island and Long Island to enter New York Bay. *Courtesy of the New York Public Library.*

just a few hundred yards from the beach, there were at least fifty unfamiliar people with unknown intentions. Before long, some of the men could be seen boarding a smaller boat, perhaps still large by Aquahonga's standards. This second boat then paddled away from the ship through the mouth of the narrows and into the wide river estuary. The first Europeans had arrived in New York Bay.[6]

The men who rowed slowly along the eastern coast of the island in 1524 were, themselves, as unfamiliar looking to Aquahonga's residents as the watercraft they sailed. The person in command, and the one likely standing out on the small bow as he surveyed the vast bay ahead of him, was Giovanni da Verrazzano, who had curly hair; light skin; and, like many in his company, sported a long, thick beard.

Verrazzano was a well-known explorer born in Florence just seven years before Columbus made his famous journey. He made his own first voyage to the New World in 1523 in the service of Francis I of France. His second voyage began the following year, when his ship, the *Dauphine*, French for "dolphin," departed the Madeira Islands on January 17, well stocked for eight months at sea. In addition to the necessary victuals, the ship carried an assortment of weapons, for sure, but also a collection of trinkets and novelties that previous voyagers had claimed the inhabitants greatly valued. The first Europeans to visit New York's sheltered harbor were prepared to deal with the natives regardless of the type of greeting they received.[7]

Luckily, Verrazzano and his men encountered no hostilities along their journey. After taking almost two months to cross the Atlantic, the ship sighted land at what would become the coast of North Carolina. Over the next few weeks, the *Dauphine* hugged the coast as it sailed north, exploring the islands and inlets of the Eastern Seaboard, all while interacting with the natives and cataloguing the flora and fauna they observed.[8]

Approximately four hundred miles north of where they first made land, the ship came on a "very pleasant situation among some steep hills, through which a very large river, deep at its mouth, forced its way to the sea."[9] As Verrazzano's log recorded, the inlet "seemed so commodious and delightful, and which we supposed must also contain great riches, as the hills showed many indications of minerals."[10]

The *Dauphine*'s logbook, which Verrazzano also transcribed in part into a long and historic letter to Francis I, records that the native peoples they encountered in the South almost always fled in fear; however, those they met as they rowed slowly along the coast of Aquahonga did not. Verrazzano found a shoreline "well-peopled" with "inhabitants…being dressed out with the feathers of birds of various colors."[11]

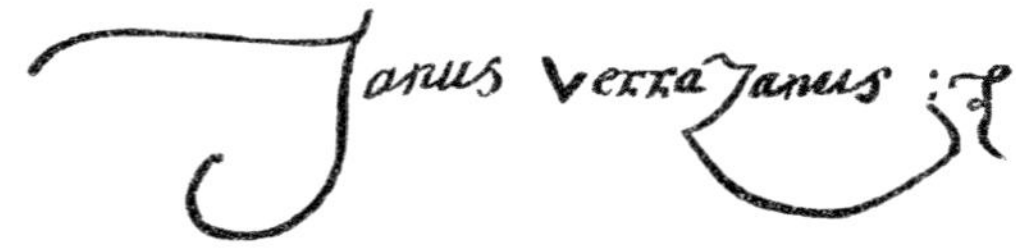

The Verrazzano Bridge recently faced a controversy over its spelling. Modern Italian uses two *z*s, but Verrazzano styled himself in Latin with only one. *From* Verrazano the Explorer *(1880).*

Instead of running away, the natives approached peacefully. "We passed up this river about half a league," the log notes, "when we found a most beautiful lake [Upper New York Bay] three leagues in circuit, upon which they were rowing thirty or more of their small boats, from one shore to the other, filled with multitudes who came to see us."[12]

In the midst of what could be described as one of the most peaceful early interactions between Europeans and Native Americans, an unlucky windstorm violently erupted on the bay. In an abundance of caution and fearful of being blown aground, Verrazzano hastily returned to the *Dauphine* to weigh its anchor and set sail for the relative safety of open water. He would never return to New York Bay and instead sailed east to make his way along the Long Island coast. For the natives left to reside on the island called Aquehonga Monocknong, it would be nearly a century before their descendants would have an encounter like the one that they had just witnessed.[13]

There is some evidence to suggest that Portuguese navigator Estavão Gomes, sailing under the patronage of Charles V of Spain, entered New York Bay during his voyage the following winter. Unfortunately, no firsthand account survives, but it is a matter of Spanish legend and hearsay that he named the Hudson River the Rio de San Antonio. Additionally, there was a claim among nineteenth-century historians that a map made by Diogo Ribeiro in 1529 was based on this voyage. It identifies a Cabo de las Arenas ("Cape of Sands") at the approximate location of Sandy Hook, New Jersey, and calls a nearby river, possibly the Hudson, the Rio de las Gamas ("River of Deer").[14] There is also archaeological evidence that European fur traders may have, at some point during the mid-1500s, visited the Hudson River Estuary. This comes in the form of European goods dated from the 1570s found at Lenape sites deep in the interior of New York State.[15] Still, there is no definitive evidence or record of these contacts, nor is there evidence that the native people who greeted Verrazzano had likewise greeted any other European in their lifetime.

Aquehonga Monocknong

Little is known about the history of Staten Island during the sixteenth and early seventeenth centuries, between the initial contact with the Europeans and when the large vessels from across the ocean returned. Prior to Verrazzano's voyage, no written history exists at all.

The Native Americans are believed to have had two names for the island, which they sometimes used together. The first, and more commonly cited, was Anglicized into Aquehonga or Aquahonga, meaning "high sandy banks."[16] The second was Monocknong, or "place of the bad woods."[17] Others claim it was the name of a specific place of refuge where the tribe could flee in defense of attacks from rival raiding parties—and later from the Dutch.[18] Neither has been accurately confirmed since their language, like most of their culture, is preserved largely through the contemporary journals of European settlers and not through their own primary written sources. However, the name does appear on the 1670 deed transferring title of the island to the Dutch.[19]

The bulk of what we understand comes from the logbooks, letters and diaries of settlers during the seventeenth century, as well as archaeological evidence that has been discovered and documented since the mid-nineteenth century.

For an island of just under sixty square miles, its pre-Columbian population has been estimated to be no more than one hundred or so permanent inhabitants,[20] and modern estimates of the entire native population around the Hudson and Delaware estuaries range between eight thousand and twelve thousand.[21] At the time of Verrazzano's encounter, the natives he met were a band known as the Raritans, which was a branch of a much broader Eastern Algonquian-speaking tribe that populated most of the coastal Northeast. This larger group is commonly referred to as the Delaware or Lenni Lenape, which roughly translates to "original people."[22]

The Raritan band, whose name now graces the river and bay that cuts through their heartland, occupied a territory ranging from the western banks of the Delaware River north of the modern city of Trenton, across the central New Jersey valleys, before ending at the marshy shores of the Atlantic and the island of Aquehonga. Furthermore, scholars believe that other Delaware bands such as the Munsee of the Hudson Valley and Iroquois traders from Upstate New York and Canada frequented the island to collect and barter for the seashells from which they could make wampum.[23]

The Lenape did not typically reside in permanent villages. Instead, they relied on seasonal campsites where they could make the most use of the resources available at any time of the year. The Raritans and other bands who resided in the coastal environment around modern New York City would typically spend the spring and early summer by the shore, where they could expect an abundance of fresh seafood in the warm tidal waters. As autumn rolled in, they would have moved inland to hunt and harvest crops, and later, they likely relocated again to a site that offered more shelter and a sure stock of firewood to brace for the cold and wet winters of the region.[24]

Throughout Aquehonga, a network of trails connected the coastal sites with inland camps and favorite hunting grounds. The main pathway traversed the island, roughly following the path of modern-day Amboy and Richmond Roads, before ending near what would become Silver Lake Park. From there, the trails circled back among the island's undulating center heights before descending again toward campsites along the Kill Van Kull and Arthur Kill.[25] The Raritans preferred to make their summer encampments in the sandier areas of the coast. Wherever sand dunes existed at the time of colonization, generations of islanders have found shell heaps, or middens, in which the remains of discarded oysters, animal bones and pottery shards were normally unearthed. Some of these can still be found today.

In addition, archaeological evidence uncovered in the nineteenth and early twentieth centuries include several larger sites, where remnants of larger refuse pits and stone tools had been found, as well as numerous human burial sites.[26] On the North Shore, during the construction of Richmond Terrace (then known as Shore Road), human remains were unearthed near the intersections of Bement and Davis Avenues, and to the east, on a portion of modern-day Corporal Thomspson Park, construction workers uncovered numerous skeletons in the typical Lenape seated burial position.[27]

In the northwest corner of the island, in the vicinity of the present-day Howland Hook Container Terminal, the Raritans had perhaps their largest and most frequently used settlement. From this spot, contact would have been easy, with the bulk of the Raritan population located to the west along New Jersey's coastal waterways and up into the Raritan River watershed. Discoveries in this neighborhood included skeletons, bone tools, stone mortars, arrowheads and beveled axes. There were also up to one hundred individual refuse pits found and multiple remnants of charred wood from years' worth of campfires.[28]

Just south, at a spot called Old Place, near the tollbooths and approaches to the Goethals Bridge, the diversity of native artifacts and burial sites indicates that it was an area used at different times throughout history.[29] In 2012, an archaeological study commissioned in advance of a gas pipeline expansion dug deeper into the earth at Old Place and uncovered new evidence—specifically a specimen of spearhead, known as a Dalton Point—that the area was used during the late Paleoindian period (around 8,500 BCE).[30]

The only other archaeological site on the island known to date as far back as this period is in Charleston at the natural gas facility formerly known as Port Mobil. There, amateur archaeologists digging in the 1950s first found Clovis points, and construction workers unearthed more as they excavated the property later. In all, nineteen fluted Clovis points were found in the vicinity by the 1980s, when large-scale construction ended,[31] giving direct evidence that humans occupied Staten Island at the same time as the mammoth, mastodon and giant beaver.[32]

Artifacts were also uncovered at different times along the Arthur Kill coastline; in the marshy necks of Chelsea and Travis; in the inlets of Fresh Kills; and in Greenridge, near the intersection of Annadale and Arthur Kill Roads. Still more was discovered in marshy areas while being cleared for farming, particularly in Huguenot, Arrochar, New Brighton, Richmondtown, Oakwood and Tompkinsville.[33]

In one notable occurrence in the late 1800s, Rossville residents Samuel and Isaac Wort were moving earth to level a knoll in their field when they discovered a stone-walled burial chamber containing the skeletal remains and adornments of several deceased Lenape. Other similar chambers were found on their property as they worked their farm throughout the years, and it is unclear what the family actually did with the remains.[34] This ancient cemetery is likely somewhere on the former Wort farm, now mostly houses on Radigan Avenue and Mason Boulevard between Rossville and Winant Avenues.[35]

Still, the most noteworthy Native American archaeological site on the island is the aptly named Burial Ridge in Tottenville, located on a wooded slope in Conference House Park just above the beach at Wards Point. The initial discovery of human remains was made on a property once owned by Joel Cole, who was taken by surprise twice while digging out foundations for his home in 1858 and 1863.[36] According to an 1874 map, the location of these since-demolished buildings was near the terminus of Clearmont Avenue, approximately 250 feet west of the present-day dog run.[37]

Some of the dozens of remains found during twentieth-century excavations at burial ridge in Conference House Park. These individuals were likely killed by arrows. *From Alanson Skinner,* The Indians of Manhattan Island and Vicinity.

The first remains that were found were that of a full skeleton and a number of separate human skulls. In the second small foundation hole, dug for an outlying building of just sixteen square feet, Cole unearthed the remains of twenty individuals. In the years immediately following, he and others found several more skeletons in the surrounding fields, both accidentally and as part of deliberate amateur digs. In the fields just north of his property, closer to the historic Conference House, excavations in 1895 uncovered ten skeletons, including one that was charred from the waist up, perhaps having met his fate by being burned at the stake.[38] These surveys, conducted by Tottenville native George M. Pepper for the American Museum of Natural History, also uncovered the body of a ten-year-old boy buried with what was described as the "richest lode of grave goods ever found in New York City."[39] Later digs on the property just south of the Cole house also yielded additional skeletons who met unpleasant ends. Skulls were found bashed open and jammed into poorly dug burial holes, and at least one was the target of several lethal arrows shot deep into his chest.[40]

By the 1960s, Burial Ridge, with its human remains and nearly five thousand artifacts had been described as the largest single indigenous archaeological site in New York.[41] In total, more than fifty digs (amateur and professional) were performed in the area between the initial discovery and the 1980s, yielding at least seventy-seven documented individual remains.[42] While the bulk of those skeletons were unearthed south of the Conference House, a significant number were found to the north, scattered in the backyards along Satterlee Street.[43]

In all, the Lenape bands who called Aquehonga home in the sixteenth century would have had a relatively prosperous and tranquil life, given the abundance of seasonal food sources, fresh water and shelter.

Unfortunately for them, there was no way to hide this abundance from the coming explorers and no changing the fact that New York Bay was replete with the natural resources so desired by the European colonists who would soon follow. From almost the moment the Dutch settled, war and bloodshed would continue. Although they would maintain a presence and be intimately involved in the island's history for over one hundred more years, the future of the Lenape culture would be forever changed in the fall of 1609.

Half Moon

It is almost impossible to think that any of the Raritans who paddled into New York Bay to greet Verrazzano in 1524 were still alive in September 1609, when a similarly dramatic scene played out on the calm water of the harbor. It is likely that the tale of the earlier encounter survived in legend and was passed down two or three generations; therefore, it is possible to surmise that those onshore watching a ship approach Staten Island through the gap between Sandy Hook and Coney Island had some inkling of who and what was on board.

Commanding the decks of the *Half Moon* was Henry Hudson, a navigator employed by the Dutch East India Company to chart an eastern passage to Asia by tacking north around Russia. Finding that path blocked by ice and unwilling to give up, he elected to sail west and, in the process, would leave his mark on the history of the New World and New York in particular.

The historical record of this journey is well documented, thanks in large part to a literate member of the crew named Robert Juet. It is unclear what duties he held on the *Half Moon* or whether his diary is the official ship's log, but we do know that Juet was an Englishman from London's East End and had sailed with Hudson in the past. This would be one of his last voyages, and he likely played a role in the 1611 mutiny that led to Hudson's death.[44]

According to his records, the ship entered Raritan Bay on September 3, 1609, finding the highlands of New Jersey and the hills of Staten Island, as well as three "rivers," which in all likelihood were the Rockaway Inlet, the Raritan River and the Narrows. Uncertain of water depths around the bay, Juet notes the ship anchored at "40 degrees 30 minutes" latitude, placing it about four miles off the Staten Island shoreline, protected from the open sea by Sandy Hook.[45]

Henry Hudson (1565–1611), an Englishman who sailed for Holland, navigated his ship, the *Half Moon*, into Raritan Bay on September 3, 1609. *New York Public Library*.

On September 4, a group of natives paddled out in their canoes and were welcomed aboard the *Half Moon*. Juet described the exchange as pleasant and civil, with the Lenape being eager to trade tobacco, corn and wheat for knives, beads and clothes.[46] The following day, Hudson sent a boat to land on the Jersey Highlands, where they again met with friendly villagers, who were eager to present them with tobacco and berries. To reciprocate, the natives were invited to the *Half Moon* that evening and came decked in their finest feather mantles. The European traders were likely more interested in the exquisite furs and copper adornments that were valuable back home.[47]

The peace was to be short-lived. On September 6, Hudson sent a five-member party north to probe the shores of Staten Island and sound the depths of the Narrows. The boat made its way along the coast, rowing into New York Bay, around the tip of the island and into the Kill Van Kull. They were almost certainly the first explorers to set their eyes on Newark Bay and the area that would become Elizabeth, New Jersey.[48] As night fell and a heavy rain set in, the crew was doubling back along the shore when they were set on by two dozen warriors in two canoes. In the ensuing skirmish, an Englishman named John Colman was shot through the throat by an arrow and died quickly, thus becoming the first European killed in hostilities in this part of the world. During a hasty retreat, the rain extinguished their boat's light, and the tidal current near the Narrows was too strong for their small anchor. After a long night of frantic paddling without any sign of the *Half Moon*, they climbed aboard its decks at ten o'clock the next morning. Hudson quickly ordered wooden planks erected along the sides of the ship as cover in an attack they expected, which thankfully did not materialize. Colman's body was transported to land and buried at a spot they coined Colman's Point,[49] which is generally assumed to be at Sandy Hook, although it's also been claimed that it's actually at Keansburg, New Jersey.

For three days, the *Half Moon* remained at anchor in Raritan Bay as the crew waited for better conditions to enter the Narrows, ever watchful of the natives who sporadically approached the boat. In one incident on September 9, two canoes paddled out from Staten Island, hoping to convince the sailors that they were interested in trading food for knives. Seeing some the occupants of one of the canoes brandishing their bows, Hudson perceived their true intent. From the account, it's unclear precisely what happened, but during a short fight, the Europeans attempted to capture three natives. Two were secured, but the third was able to make a desperate leap into the bay.[50]

On September 12, Hudson maneuvered the *Half Moon* deftly through the Narrows and recalibrated his ship to the north. For the most part, the natives he encountered heading up the river bore no animosity, and Juet's journal records shared meals and the exchange of goods and food on several occasions.[51] Along the way, near the modern city of Kingston, the two captives from Aquehonga who had been held on board for nearly a week were able to slip out to shore through a porthole. From here they gleefully shouted taunts back at the ship. After ten days, the *Half Moon* reached a shallow stretch of river, likely between Albany and Troy, where the captain discovered they could sail on no farther.[52]

On the journey downriver, somewhere around the Hudson Highlands, the ship was covertly approached by a canoe, and one of its passengers scrambled up the rudder board and in through a cabin window. Juet recalled the native grabbing "my Pillow, and two Shirts, and two Bandeleers"[53] before he was shot in the chest and killed by a crewmember. The *Half-Moon*'s rowboat was launched in pursuit of the others, some of whom fled by canoe as others swam toward shore. Suddenly, one of the warriors in the water grabbed ahold of the boat and tried to overturn it, until the ship's cook "tooke a Sword, and cut off one of his hands, and he was drowned."[54]

The *Half Moon* had numerous encounters with Native Americans from Staten Island and throughout the Hudson River Valley. Some interactions were peaceful, and some were not. *Library of Congress.*

On the afternoon of October 2, after traveling about thirty miles, the *Half Moon* was at anchor along the shore near the present-day Bronx. Suddenly, a Lenape war party approached in two canoes led by one of the two Staten Island natives who had escaped from the ship two weeks before. Sensing the fight, Hudson and his crew immediately took defensive positions. They were quickly proven right as the warriors maneuvered their canoes off the ship's stern and let loose a volley of arrows. In response, Hudson ordered a volley of musket fire, which "killed two or three of them." Another group of warriors, which the account estimates at over one hundred men, stood on a nearby embankment in preparation for another attack. Juet manned the ship's light cannon and fired off a round in their direction, killing two. Another canoe of ten men approached, and Juet again fired the cannon, this time killing just one before a volley of musketry struck several more.[55]

Hudson left New York Bay without any further mention of the land around the Narrows and promptly returned to England. From there, he sent a dispatch to the Dutch regarding the wealth of natural resources in the areas he explored, with a request that they outfit him for another voyage. The English, however, desired his services as well and forbade his return to the New World under a Dutch flag.[56] He would never again see the river that now bears his name.

Hudson's account did have its desired effect, though, and the Dutch were keenly interested in returning to the bays, inlets and rivers of what would become New York Harbor. This included the scar of land that the *Half Moon*'s crew identified and presumed was surrounded by water, and which they referred to as Staaten Eylandt in honor of the States-General of Holland, the Dutch parliament, under whose ensign the boat sailed.[57]

The short period following Hudson's voyage was not particularly eventful in the history of Staten Island. The Raritans, perhaps fearful of another violent encounter and perceiving the long-term danger, were said to have constructed signal stations at the high points of the island, including one at Fort Wadsworth and another at Todt Hill, but no direct evidence of this survives.[58] However, the merchants who followed Hudson came with great eagerness for trade and relatively benign intentions, spurred on by the profits to be made from exchanging trivial items for the furs that were then in high demand at home.

In 1610, a hopeful Dutch ship anchored off the Narrows to attempt a trade. The Raritans amassed themselves on the shore in defense, and all efforts at brokering a friendly summit fell through. Instead, the ship traveled north and conducted its business with the Mohawks of the upper Hudson,[59] likely helping to expedite the establishment of Fort Nassau, a permanent trading post on Castle Island near Albany, just a short time thereafter.[60]

Over the next few years, a number of competing Dutch captains visited the New York Harbor area, including Cornelis May (after whom Cape May, New Jersey, is named) and Adriaen Block, who first charted the island now bearing his name and was first to use the term "New Netherland" to describe the Dutch claims between English Virginia and French Canada.[61] For the most part, the lucrative efforts were led by Hendrick Christiaensen, who entered the many inlets of New York Bay and traded with the natives wherever he could, including in Staten Island.[62] These successful voyages only furthered interest in Holland, and in 1614, the States-General set up the United New Netherland Company to hold a monopoly of the Dutch fur trade in the New World. The charter lasted just three years and was not renewed. However, in 1621, the government granted the fur trade and all other rights to a larger and more heavily capitalized new firm, the Dutch West India Company, which would have jurisdiction over all Dutch trade in West Africa and the Americas, including New Netherland.[63] The colonization of New York, and in particular the island that guards the entrance to its harbor, was about to begin.

By winter of that year, the few traders of New Netherland had sent fifty thousand guilders' worth of pelts back to Holland, along with exaggerated reports of the region's abundance and wealth. The company responded the following year by sending more than one hundred new colonists, along with the livestock, supplies and tools needed to establish a permanent foothold. The cattle were put to pasture on Manhattan, where land was cleared for farming, and on its southern tip, a site was chosen for Fort Amsterdam, the first large stone-and-earth fortification in the harbor.[64]

2

STAATEN EYLANDT

The Dutch West India Company's attempts to settle New Netherland began in earnest in the summer of 1624, when Cornelis May, its first director, captained the *Nieu Nederlandt* and its cargo of thirty families through the Narrows and into Upper New York Bay. May was determined that these settlers fan out over the expanse of the colony, sending families far away to its eastern and western boundaries to populate the Connecticut and Delaware Rivers. The bulk, however, he sent up the North (Hudson) River to reestablish the lucrative fur trade near Albany, where Fort Nassau had been destroyed by a flood a few years earlier. The new post, called Fort Orange, was settled by eighteen enterprising families and was soon managing a successful trade with the nearby Mahicans, who were generally well disposed to the Dutch and eager to do business. Finally, May ordered a small contingent of settlers to occupy Governor's Island, and at least one farm was established on Manhattan Island.[65]

The bulk of these original "Dutch" families who settled in the earliest years may not have been very Dutch at all. The majority were Walloons from the Low Country provinces that form part of modern Belgium (Hainault, Namur, Liege, Luxembourg and South Brabant).[66] This group was descended from the original Celtic inhabitants of ancient Gaul and were culturally and linguistically related to the French. In fact, a study of 904 immigrants arriving during the period of Dutch rule found that almost half had origins outside of the traditional Dutch provinces.[67]

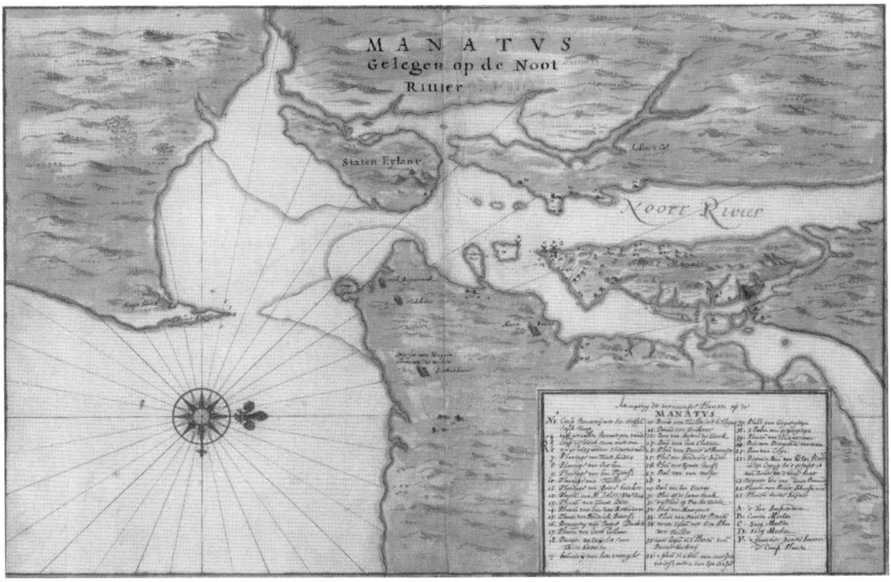

This map is believed to be the work of Joan Vinckeboons in 1639 and is perhaps the first one to name Staten Island. *Library of Congress.*

The Walloons who sailed in 1624 and 1625 were Protestant, and many had suffered during the generational devastation of the Thirty Years' War and other European wars of religion.[68] They initially applied to the English Virginia Company for permission to establish a settlement there in 1621, but after requesting a degree of autonomy, self-governance and, most importantly, free transportation, they were rejected. Thus, they were forced to make a second appeal to the powers in Amsterdam, who were less inclined and in less of a position to set conditions.[69]

It is unclear if there were any attempts to launch a settlement on Staten Island in these earliest days. Both J.J. Clute's *Annals of Staten Island* and Richard Bayle's *History of Richmond County* make reference to a Sarah Rapelje, who is alleged to have been the first European birth in New Amsterdam, as she was born while her family was temporarily on Staten Island.[70] However, it is more likely that she was born at Fort Orange, where her parents first landed,[71] or at Wallabout Bay (the name derived from *Waale boght*, meaning Walloon's Bay), where her family eventually settled and became the first residents of Brooklyn.[72]

Whether or not any attempts were made to inhabit Staten Island in the 1620s and 1630s is a subject for debate; however, it was routinely explored

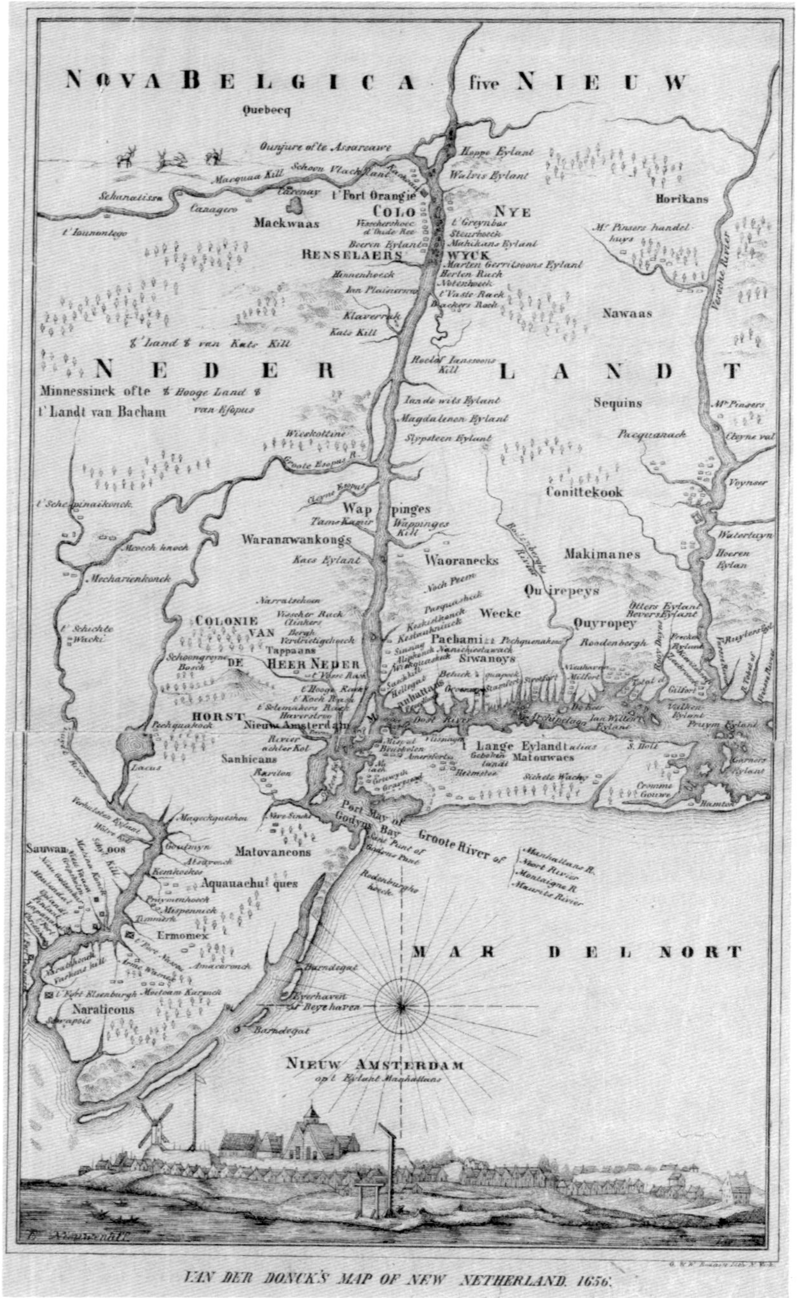

This map, included in Adrian van der Donck's *Description of New Netherland* (1655), is one of the first detailed maps of the Dutch colony. *New York Public Library.*

by the Dutch and its abundant resources were presumably used. In one of the earliest written accounts of the colony, Adriaen van der Donck described the common practice of departing Dutch ships stopping on the island: "The outward bound ships usually stop at the watering place under Staten Island, to lay in a sufficient supply of wood and water, which are easily obtained at that place."[73]

Van der Donck had arrived in New Amsterdam in 1642 and completed his writing by 1653, but from the context of his writing, it sounds as though this practice had long been customary. The watering place" is therefore one of the earliest specific locations on the island that historians can attach to a recorded description. The spot was marked with a bronze tablet by the Daughters of the American Revolution in 1925, and it still stands in Tompkinsville Park at the intersection of Bay Street and Victory Boulevard.[74]

PATROONS AND PROBLEMS

In its first five years, the Dutch West India Company faced a fundamental question: whether New Netherland would develop as a permanent settlement or as a series of temporary factory outposts existing for the sole purpose of acquiring and processing pelts. Among its directors, there was a clear division of opinions, while in practice, the company seemed to pursue both courses simultaneously. The original 1624 Provisional Orders, which set the colony's regulations, prioritized the output of the company factories over the will and desire of the settlers, while at the same time, it also allowed them to form a council and retain a degree of self-government. By 1626, this council, along with Peter Minuit as the newly named director, became the established authority in the land and was on its way toward providing long-term residents.[75]

That spring, one of Minuit's first formal actions was to embark on a policy of purchasing the lands around New York Bay from the various Lenape groups who inhabited them. While no deed survives, the legendary story of Manhattan's purchase for twenty-four dollars (sixty guilders) is memorialized in a report by the company's liaison to Amsterdam in November 1626.[76] Earlier in the year there is also a record of Staten Island's purchase of a collection of cloth, kettles, axes, hoes, wampum and other trinkets.[77] Regardless, the Dutch still hesitated to make any attempt to formally settle the island immediately thereafter.

To modern New Yorkers, it may seem on the surface that Minuit's development and expansion of early New Amsterdam was successful. However, it was not seen in the same light by the powerbrokers of the West India Company, who had him recalled by 1633.[78] The profits from the pelt trade were slowly declining as New Netherland's relationship with critical native trading partners soured, and the price dropped as the supply of products from elsewhere within Holland's reach became more easily accessible. The company faced a choice: change direction or let the whole experiment go belly-up.[79]

This financial crisis gave an opportunity to the faction that favored the long-term settlement of New Netherland, as it became all too clear that hired labor alone could not sustain the outposts scattered about the colony. Led by Kiliaen van Rennselaer, an Amsterdam diamond merchant, they were able to convince the company to grant large swaths of New Netherland to patroons who committed to purchase additional land from the natives and bear the costs of populating it with more than fifty immigrants. Van Rennselaer was the first to apply and receive his "patroonship," which amounted to a 700,000-acre tract of land near Fort Orange called Rennselaerswyck,[80] including all of modern Rennselaer County.

In exchange for bearing some of the costs, patroons were granted a limited degree of autonomy from the company's director in New Amsterdam. They were permitted a minimum of one mile of waterfront, where they could establish their own coastal trade and set up local governments and courts with approval from the New Netherland council.[81]

After van Rennselaer, others were quick to apply. In 1630, Michel Pauw was granted the patroonship he called Pavonia, consisting of the western shores of the Hudson River south of modern Hoboken, which, if one pictures the river emptying out through the Narrows, included Staten Island.[82] On August 10, the purchase of Aquehonga was formalized in writing by the director, who exchanged a "certain lot of merchandise" for it from a group of Raritan elders named Krahorat, Tamehap, Totenackwemama, Wieromics, Sicarewach, Sackwewew, Wissipoack and Saheinsios, all "inhabitants, owners and inheritors of the island called by us Staten Island."[83]

Whatever dreams of Pavonia that Pauw may have had, they did not materialize. Nor did he make any earnest attempt to colonize Staten Island. Although he did manage to build a house on the site of present-day Jersey City, his patroonship failed to generate any income.[84] In 1637, he sold the land, which he originally paid nothing for, back to the West India Company for twenty-six thousand guilders.[85]

The next attempt to establish a settlement on the island saw only slightly more success. In 1636, van Rennselaer's nephew Wooter van Twiller was in his third year of his directorship of New Amsterdam.[86] That year, he granted Staten Island to David Pietersz de Vries, who wrote in his journal that he "wished to return and plant a colony upon it."[87] By January 1639, de Vries began the work needed to establish a permanent settlement for a small group of families.[88] The precise location of this town is not known, but it is generally assumed to be north of Rosebank, where settlers could have made quick work of building shelters from split planks and bark into the side of the hills.[89]

Van Twiller's tenure as director of New Netherland was short-lived, and he was fired in 1637. Contemporary accounts claim he was preoccupied with self-serving land grabs and spent the majority of his time inebriated. The directors in Amsterdam hoped to unravel his administration and

David Pietersz de Vries (1593–1662) was granted Staten Island in 1636 and attempted to make a settlement near Rosebank in 1639 before his land patent was annulled. *New York Public Library.*

eventually annulled the grants of land he had authorized to his allies. Instead of honoring the titles, they sought to offer these large tracts outside of New Amsterdam to a fresh wave of emigrants, who would be offered cheap transportation, a schoolmaster for their children and the ability to practice free trade in the colony.[90]

It was during this wave of migration in 1639, when Cornelis Melyn, a wealthy merchant from Antwerp, was authorized to take possession of Staten Island and expand its sparse development.[91] De Vries's journal records the awkwardness he felt when Melyn finally disembarked on shore in 1641: "The ship Oak Tree arrived here, in which came a person named Melyn, who said that Staten Island belonged to him, that it was given by the directors to him… which I could not believe, as I had sailed in the year thirty-eight to take possession of said island, and had settled my men upon it. I thought better things of the directors than this."[92]

The dispute was settled when Melyn received de Vries's consent to colonize a portion of Staten Island near Fort Wadsworth, where the Lenape had long cleared fields for corn. He established a farming community of several families and built a blockhouse and signal station that could be seen from New Amsterdam and warn of approaching ships. On June 19, 1642, the directors formally presented Melyn with letters of patent granting him the title of patroon of Staten Island and ownership of its entirety, with the stipulation that a farm be reserved for de Vries. Sadly, however, the dispute with his fellow settler would not prove to be the biggest problem involving Staten Island that both men had to face.

KIEFT'S WAR

In 1638, van Twiller's replacement took his first steps on the docks running along New Amsterdam's shoreline. Willem Kieft, a merchant with limited experience in governing, was rumored to have questionable business practices and likely received his appointment as director due to his family's well-heeled connections in the Netherlands. It was on his order that Melyn

Opposite: This mural is just one among the collection at Borough Hall that tell the story of the county's history. It is titled *Cornelius Melyn Trades with the Indians* and celebrates the first patroon of Staten Island. *Courtesy of Peter Trivelas.*

Left: During the early settlement of New Netherland, the relationship between traders and Native Americans went somewhat smoothly. That changed under Director Willem Kieft. *Library of Congress.*

constructed the signaling station, a significant first for New Amsterdam. He also established a distillery on Staten Island in 1640, earning the honor of being the first in New Netherland and arguably all of the future United States.[93] That said, by the end of his time in office, Staten Island would be laid to waste, and those colonists who managed to survive would be huddled for protection with many others in the safety of Fort Amsterdam. As will happen many times in the island's future, poor decisions from those governing from Manhattan proved disastrous for its inhabitants.

The trouble started in 1640, when a ship of the West India Company, en route to its holdings in the Delaware watershed, made a stop at Staten Island's Watering Place to take on supplies for the journey. It is believed that the crew of this ship, seeing no other people on the island or anywhere in the vicinity, stole a number of pigs from the nearby de Vries farm.[94]

Whether Kieft had any proof of who the real culprits were is unknown. His accounts died with him in a shipwreck while on his way to Amsterdam to defend his record. However, he saw the incident as an opportunity to settle a score with the troublesome Lenapes, especially the Raritans, who had previously tried to impede Dutch interests. Earlier that year, they had sent a trading party scurrying off Staten Island in a hail of arrows, and they were involved in killing livestock and damaging property elsewhere around the bay. They were also unwilling to go along with Kieft's preposterous and extortive new policy of demanding tribute from the various local tribal groups in exchange for "protection."[95]

The director's response was to order his provincial secretary, Cornelius van Twienhoven, and seventy men to invade the territorial lands of the Raritans, destroy their crops and capture any warriors they could. However, after finding that burning crops and villages was unsatisfactory, the troops became enraged and insubordinate and exceeded the authority they were given.[96] Van Twienhoven's efforts to rein them in were ignored, and they wantonly killed all those they saw, including the brother of a sachem,[97] who was tortured "in his private parts with a piece of split wood" before his execution.[98]

The response was unsurprisingly harsh and swift. "The 1st of September my men on Staten Island were killed by the Indians and the Raritans," de Vries recalled. During the attack, the Raritan warriors made it known that they, too, were aware of the false charges of theft leveled against them by the new director. "Thus I lost the beginning of my colony on Staten Island, through the conduct of Commander Kieft, who wished to charge upon the savages what his own people had done," concluded de Vries.[99]

This didn't stop Kieft from pursuing his course, and he quickly placed a target on those Lenape residing on Staten Island, enlisting the help of nearby Munsee bands in the effort. He is said to have offered "ten fathoms of wampum for the head of a Raritan, and twenty fathoms of wampum for the head of every Indian engaged in the murders upon Staten Island."[100] Two months later, Kieft, alongside a sachem of the Tankitekes, another Dutch-allied tribal band, confronted de Vries outside of Fort Amsterdam. As a sign of respect for the Europeans, the sachem presented both men with the severed hand of "the chief who had killed or shot with arrows" de Vries's murdered farm workers.[101] The token of revenge was accepted, and the Raritans concluded a cease-fire with Kieft in 1641.[102] However, the truce did not quell the bloodshed for long or satisfy Kieft's desire to continue exacting punishment on the Raritans for that incident, as well as other murders that had occurred.

On February 25, 1643, over the objections of de Vries and many others, Kieft ordered a major attack on the enemy natives encamped at Pavonia on

Director Willem Kieft (1597–1647) was responsible for a series of poor decisions that resulted in the destruction of the earliest settlements on Staten Island. *Library of Congress.*

the opposite bank of the Hudson, while another company struck those just to the north at Corlear's Hook.[103] By the next morning, the extent of the butchery was clear to those awaiting word in New Amsterdam:

> *When it was day the soldiers returned to the fort, having massacred or murdered eighty Indians, and considering they had done a deed of Roman valor, in murdering so many in their sleep; where infants were torn from their mother's breasts, and hacked to pieces in the presence of the parents, and the pieces thrown into the fire and in the water, and other sucklings, being bound to small boards, were cut, stuck, and pierce, and miserably massacred in a manner to move a heart of stone. Some were thrown into the river, and when the fathers and mothers endeavored to save them the soldiers would not let them come on land but made both parents and children drown.*[104]

Within weeks of these attacks, the colony was prepared for an all-out war. The Lenape groups organized themselves to collectively fight the Dutch, attacking and burning outlying settlements across the entirety of New Netherland, while the majority of Europeans outside of New Amsterdam abandoned their homes for the safety of the city. With only a few hundred men able to bear arms, the colony sent a desperate, but unrealized, appeal for support to Holland. In the short term, however, they were able to broker a deal with their neighbors in New England to secure the assistance of a small contingent of troops for the winter of 1643–44, all veterans of that colony's Pequot War years earlier.[105]

The combined Dutch and New England forces launched several attacks on Lenape villages in Connecticut, Westchester and Long Island.[106] On Staten Island, in one of the last actions of the conflict, forty Dutchmen under the command of Captain Jochem Pietersen[107] and thirty-five Englishmen under Lieutenant George Baxter completed an all-nighter to surprise the Raritans at Mariner's Harbor. However, as day broke, they found the village had already been abandoned in a hasty retreat and had to settle on burning the crops and homes.[108]

Kieft's war ended in 1645. Soon after, his directorship did too but not before some sixteen hundred Native Americans and dozens of colonists had died and settlements on Staten Island and elsewhere were in ruin. His misguided attempts to wring tribute from the natives had nearly brought the entire colony to its knees. Kieft's war also opened the door to a new challenge: in its new weakened state, New Amsterdam was now an easy target for English imperialism.[109] He was recalled to Holland to account for his failures.

NEW DIRECTOR, NEW SETTLEMENTS

When Peter Stuyvesant and his new bride, Judith Bayard, arrived in New Amsterdam in 1647, the city was still recovering from the conflict. Years of attacks and crop burnings had left the countryside in tatters, and all but a few of the settlers had abandoned their farms and fled to the collective protection of the city.[110]

Stuyvesant immediately took steps to restore order and embarked on a series of reforms and new ordinances. His goal was to have New Amsterdam mimic the well-ordered towns of the Low Countries that immigrants would have been used to. During his tenure, the population of New Netherland would climb to 3,500 in the mid-1650s and almost 9,000 by 1664. He was aided by an aggressive advertising campaign that lured colonists with promises of easily cultivated land and, equally important, a more liberal set of freedoms than what was standard elsewhere. Additionally, the loss of the prized colony of Brazil to the Portuguese in 1654 caused the Dutch States-General and West India Company to refocus all of their colonial efforts on their final possession in the New World.[111]

For the patroon of Staten Island, Stuyvesant's directorship proved both challenging and controversial, and to say that he and Melyn did not see eye to eye would be an understatement. Their principal disagreement regarded Melyn's frequent habit of disparaging the government of New Netherland and demanding new investigations of the previous director. Stuyvesant did not like the government's authority being questioned under any circumstance and believed that private citizens like Melyn lacked the authority to investigate the colony's appointed leaders.

As a result, the director had the patroon banished, and as fate would have it, he was on the *Princess Amelia*, the same ship taking the recalled Kieft to Amsterdam. As the ship approached the Welsh coast, its captain mistook the Bristol Channel for the English Channel, and it ran aground and sunk. Of the two, only Melyn survived.[112]

Back in Holland, the indomitable patroon would not be deterred. The West India Company eventually reversed Melyn's banishment, and he began raising money "to restock my ruined colony."[113] To accomplish this, he partnered with Henderick van der Capellan, who invested significant capital in exchange for one-third of the island. The two outfitted a ship, the *Netherland Fortune*, which set out for Staten Island in 1650 with seventy people. Somewhere in the Atlantic, the ship hit a ran of bad weather that nearly cost the lives of all on board. They almost run out of food and water before finding a welcome refuge and the availability of provisions in the English colony of Rhode Island.[114]

The stroke of bad luck dissuaded neither Melyn nor his cargo from their effort to colonize Staten Island, and when the *Netherland Fortune* arrived on its shores on December 19, the passengers "joyfully went on land, thanking God for having been freed from the water and the ship."[115] By 1651, they had laid out sixteen farms, twenty-seven buildings and a herd of plow oxen and milk cows.[116] We know from contemporary accounts that this collection of houses, barns and cleared pastures could be seen from the harbor along a gentle rise in the land just below the island's steep hills and was likely near the modern neighborhoods of Stapleton and Clifton.[117] The initial success of this little idyllic hamlet caused Melyn to boast, "Even to those arriving from [Manhattan] itself, were surprised at the large crop of grain which had this year been produced through our diligence....Every thing began to be abundant on Staten Island."[118]

While things seemed to be going well for the time being, Melyn's continued feud with Stuyvesant consumed much of his energy and personal wealth. Rather than the semiautonomous and almost feudal land rights patroons expected to have,[119] Melyn simply could not unbind himself from the burdensome director in New Amsterdam.

In 1651, the patroon of Staten Island was summoned to appear in the city to answer for new charges leveled against him by Stuyvesant.[120] The allegation was that he seditiously acted against the director and the West India Company with hostile tribes and was said to have embezzled weapons.[121]

A stalemate ensued, and Melyn refused to appear and face charges he knew to be false. For that, the director confiscated his land and buildings in New Amsterdam, and Meyln resolved to remain as far away as possible in his colony on Staten Island. Before leaving Holland the year before, the Dutch directors furnished him with a "safe conduct," essentially allowing him to return to his work on the island free of harassment from the New Amsterdam government.[122] Knowing Melyn was armed with what essentially amounted to a get-out-of-jail-free card, Stuyvesant was hesitant to use force to bring him to town against his will. With one exception in 1655, when Melyn appeared in New Amsterdam and was jailed for twenty-five days, the director would not make any attempts to enforce his court summonses and judgments against the patroon for fear of the reaction from the company's leadership in Holland.[123]

The stalemate did not mean Stuyvesant made any effort to support Melyn in growing his colony, and to some degree, the patroonship operated autonomously from New Amsterdam. From roughly 1650 to 1655, things were going well. Crops were growing, cattle were grazing and the small population of Staten Island was prospering. Melyn's risky venture began to pay off, and years later, he would recall, "Through God's blessing I again began to recover my losses."[124] But once again, for the patroon and his domain, the luck would be short-lived.

In 1655, Stuyvesant led a convoy of four armed ships and a few hundred soldiers into to the Delaware and Schuylkill Rivers, where encroaching fur traders and tobacco farmers from the colony of New Sweden had set up a string of trading posts and settlements. From there, they began regular harassment of Dutch merchants operating on the southern frontier of New Netherland. The sortie succeeded, and the Swedes gave up without firing a shot. Unfortunately, there was no time to celebrate. One hundred miles away from home, Stuyvesant received the first letters informing him of renewed bloodshed with the natives.[125]

On September 15, 1655, sixty-four canoes and nearly six hundred warriors from tribes throughout the Hudson Valley descended on New York Bay to raid rival Canarsie Indians on southern Long Island. Along the way, they put to shore near the southern tip of Manhattan. One of their women began foraging for food and stopped to collect peaches from an orchard belonging to Hendrick van Dijck, located on what was then called Heare Straet, now Broadway. Van Dijck caught her in the act and killed her instantly, thus starting the conflict known as the Peach War. The response from the warriors was instant and deadly. One of van Dijck's neighbors, Paulus Leendertsz van der Grift, was struck in the head with a tomahawk as he rushed to his friend's defense. Soon, the raiding party descended through New Amsterdam, ransacking houses and terrifying the inhabitants before a militia was organized by Cornelis van Tienhoven to force them away.[126]

Days later, the natives took the fight to the shores of Staten Island, which had been left unguarded as the soldiers who garrisoned the blockhouse and signal station were either with Stuyvesant's convoy to the south or still in New Amsterdam from the night before. With such few men bearing arms, the outcome was not pleasant.[127]

First, the raiders attacked the main cluster of houses, along with their haystacks and grain stores. The smoldering remains were visible to passing ships for weeks. The besieged townspeople sought refuge at the patroon's estate, but the natives eventually found them and set fire to all of its buildings as well. According to Melyn, as "cinders began to fall down on us,"[128] he and his band were forced to fight their way out and managed to make a hasty retreat to an outlying house along the shoreline. There they held out all night, hoping the fires and noise would alert the soldiers across the bay at New Amsterdam. As the hours passed, so did any hope of reinforcements.[129]

Luckily, the natives did not burn down the house and instead demanded that the colonists surrender and face capture. With no other option, Melyn accepted the terms. The fifty-one survivors were kept in captivity for over a month while their captors demanded a ransom, "which was to be paid if we did not want to be burnt alive in a fire which for this purpose had been already prepared and was burning."[130] In all, sixteen Staten Islanders were killed, including Melyn's son, son-in-law and two nephews. Twenty-five houses and barns were burned. Cattle and crops were destroyed.[131] The borough's first little town was in ashes—the result of a conflict it had little to do with.

Melyn fled. With nothing left on Staten Island and the risk of imprisonment in New Amsterdam, he and his family sought and received protection in the English colony of New Haven. In 1660, he returned to Holland to try to recoup his investment from the West India Company. He obtained recompense for losses caused by the Peach War; however, his title to the entirety of Staten Island was finished. After his death in 1661, his son Jacob would continue to press the Dutch, then later the English authorities, and would eventually regain ownership of the portion of property that his father had cleared and cultivated.[132]

His partner, van der Capellan, did not immediately give up hope that the small colony on Staaten Eylandt could be revived. This time, however, he would have to do it without any support whatsoever from Peter Stuyvesant and the government of New Amsterdam.

Through his agent, Captain Adriaen Post, van der Capellan began to resettle some of the surviving colonists in 1656. That year, he also tried to entice new ones with the prospect of cheap land grants in exchange for a pledge of allegiance to him over Stuyvesant and New Amsterdam. Both efforts failed miserably.

The director and New Netherland Council took issue with the plan, specifically stating that maintaining a garrison on the island was simply not worth the cost compared to its meager agricultural return. When Post petitioned for more soldiers in 1659, Stuvesant refused, saying, "As very few persons live on Staten Island…not more than two or three families, for whose safety pursuant to your orders five or six soldiers are kept at the expense of the Company and as so far no more show any inclination to settle there as colonists."[133]

Van der Capellan's efforts to deal with the natives on his own met with similar results. In the hope of preventing attacks, his attorney negotiated a new purchase of the island and signed a peace treaty with the Raritans on July 10, 1657. Unfortunately, the goods that were offered as payment never arrived from Holland, and since the Lenape did not receive them, they refused to move off the land.[134] By December, the directors in Holland, who believed all agreements to purchase land must come across their desks, annulled the deal regardless. They ordered Director Stuyvesant to void the transfer and negotiate Staten Island from the natives by himself.[135]

There was little opposition, because in 1659, Stuyvesant was notified of the death of Hendrick van der Capellan, and the following year, his heirs surrendered all claim to his lands. With both Melyn and van der Capellan gone, Staten Island fell into the hands of the West India Company and Stuyvesant's government in New Amsterdam.[136]

The Huguenots

With Melyn and van der Capellan's efforts ended, Staten Island was likely void of any permanent European residents by 1660. The last Dutch land patent from this period is to Johannes de Decker, who first emigrated from Holland to New Netherland in 1655 and held a number of official positions for the company over the next decade. On January 15, 1664, he was granted 120 acres on the island, the specific location of which is unknown. De Decker would come to play an active role in the English conquest of Fort Orange and all of New Netherland and would be one of the six signers of the Articles of Capitulation.[137]

De Decker would also prove to be an enemy of the early English government, and as we shall subsequently see, the overall conquest had a tumultuous effect on all of the few families on Staten Island. Shortly after the surrender, though, he was discovered in the process of organizing a rebellion in the northern Hudson Valley and was promptly banished from the colony by the English. Years later, no earlier than 1670, he was allowed to return and retire to his farm on Staten Island. And although he would eventually become the progenitor of a prominent family who still claims descendants in the borough (and whose name survives with Decker Farm and Decker Avenue), it cannot be said that it was he who established its first surviving permanent settlement.[138]

To that honor, Staten Island, like all of New Netherland really, finds its origins in the fallout from the armed conflicts of the Reformation in Europe. Traditional Dutch tolerance of religions and the West India Company's general acceptance of diverse settlers resulted in a large heterogeneous society in the colony. To those fleeing the religious wars on the Continent, it seemed like an attractive option. By 1664, New Amsterdam's diversity was on full display and was home to Walloons, English, French, Swedes, Irish, Scots and Africans, as well as Anglicans, Quakers, Anabaptists, Presbyterians, Catholics and Jews.[139]

The Huguenots were French Calvinists, predominately from northern France near the Low Countries and the western coastal city of La Rochelle.

In the surviving records of New Netherland, it is important to note that the term *Huguenot* was not applied, but instead, French Protestants were often labeled as Walloons, differentiated only by their place of origin.[140]

The persecution of French Protestants and unrest over their status in France began in the late 1550s and essentially continued for over one hundred years. In 1598, Huguenots saw signs of progress when a somewhat sympathetic Henry IV issued the Edict of Nantes, granting them religious freedoms. However, his grandson Louis XIV spent a bulk of his reign chipping away at those rights and sanctioning new persecutions.[141] Those came into full force in the 1681 Dragonnades, a policy of billeting dragoons in Protestant communities with the goal of bullying them into conversion. This would eventually culminate in Louis's 1685 revocation of the Edict of Nantes itself.

Thousands were killed throughout this long period of oppression, including 20,000 as part of the 1572 St. Bartholomew's Day Massacre alone. By the end of Louis XIV's reign, 150,000 Huguenots had fled the country for safer domicile as far as Scandinavia, South Africa and the Americas.[142]

Huguenot emigration out of France came in two significant waves. The *Premier Refuge* occurred in a relatively small number and coincided with a continental diaspora of Europe's Protestants and included some of the earliest settlers on Staaten Eylandt. The second, or *Grand Refuge*, was larger and populated the Western Hemisphere with thousands of French immigrants after the revocation of the edict, again including many

An 1854 *Harper's Monthly* interpretation of the landing of Walloon families in New Netherland. *New York Public Library.*

immigrants to the island. By 1710, approximately 200,000 of France's 730,000 Protestants had left.[143]

Since the earliest days of the West India Company's operation in New Netherland, Huguenot names were found among passenger manifests and in colonial records. In 1650, they made up one-fifth of all settlers and were a part of the repeated settlement attempts by Melyn, de Vries and van der Capellan.[144]

In 1661, Stuyvesant granted a petition from nineteen settlers, who hoped to make a new crack at colonizing Staten Island. His interest in doing so wasn't grounded in the belief that the island was more valuable than before or less prone to native attacks. Rather, it was largely in response to a growing threat from the English. The West India Company and the States-General had become nervous that English incursions and settlements on eastern Long Island were merely a precursor to a larger invasion in the future and urged the director to fortify his positions around the bay.[145] If the island wasn't useful for agriculture, its position guarding the harbor certainly could be advantageous to New Amsterdam's defense.

In response, Stuyvesant spurred the development of small hamlets on both sides of the Narrows, each with a garrisoned blockhouse to safeguard the entrance to the bay. The larger of the two was on Long Island, where the village of New Utrecht was formed in the 1650s by Cornelius van Wreckhoven and Jaques Cortelyou. They managed to subdivide the land into twenty fifty-acre plots,[146] and by the mid-1660s, it had about twenty-four families in all.[147]

In late 1661 and early 1662, the complementary settlement on the opposite side of the Narrows was formed just out of sight of New Amsterdam on the south side of the island's hilly rise. After two years, Stuyvesant boasted that it "has now about 12 to 14 families of Dutch and French from the Palatinate"[148] (a region of southwest Germany home to many Protestants).[149] Among these first permanent pioneers of Staten Island were many whose names would be memorialized in the borough's twentieth-century street names, including Walraven Luten, Pieter Wynant and Pierre Billiou, who would go on to play a significant role in the settlement's political and civic life.[150]

The exact site of the town they founded is not presently marked in any meaningful way. Stuyvesant recorded only that "it lies about half an hours walk from the Narrows, there being no more convenient place for a village near the water."[151] Twentieth-century historians placed it in what would be considered Arrochar or South Beach, at a "rectangular bend in the Old

Town Road near St. Mary's Cemetery."[152] That portion of Old Town Road was later changed to Quintard Street, but the bend still exists where it meets Ledyard Place—now the site of auto body shops and warehouses.[153] After several years, this settlement became known as Oude Dorp, which is Dutch for "Old Town," and was used to differentiate it from later Dutch and Huguenot hamlets farther south along Fresh Kills and at Great Kills.

The area proved well suited for agricultural endeavors. Its general topography was flat, and the fields were likely already cleared by generations of Raritan slash-and-burn corn farming. To the north, where the earth gradually rises through the neighborhoods of Dongan Hills and Concord, the settlers would have found pristine pastures for grazing cattle and swine.[154] It was around this time and in that very neighborhood that Pierre Billiou constructed the oldest part of the landmarked Billiou-Stillwell-Perine house, located at 1476 Richmond Road. It remains the oldest building in the borough.[155]

The growing town also had ample fresh water and access to a cornucopia of sea life in the adjacent salt marshes. These were fed through a series of streams and creeks that still feed the New Creek Bluebelt, named for Peter Noue,[156] who arrived in the settlement in 1663 on board the *Spotted Cow*, along with another wave of French Protestants.[157]

The subsequent Huguenot immigrants, like Noue, did not confine themselves to Old Town and its vicinity. In 1665, Daniel Perrin settled on the South Shore and eventually amassed eighty acres. Other locals referred to him as "the Huguenot," a name that stayed with the neighborhood that developed near his estate. A decade later, Jacques Guyon settled along Crescent Beach in Great Kills, where other French and Dutch settlers soon followed. The Cortelyou family established a farm along Fresh Kills at Greenridge, near the modern avenue of the same name. Huguenots were also part of the founding of Cockles Town, the original name of Richmondtown, where Samuel Grasset established a tannery using the water of the Kills,[158] and where public meetings, Bible reading and schooling eventually took place at the Voorlezer's house. In Dutch, a *Voorlezer* is one who reads the Bible aloud and educates children, and this building, now in the possession of Historic Richmondtown, had long been believed to be the oldest known schoolhouse in America.[159] This theory was proven incorrect in 2018, after the publication of a Historic Structure Report, which used archaeological evidence and dendrochronology to conclude that the current structure is not the original but is probably a reconstruction completed in the mid-1700s.[160] However, what is likely Staten Island's second-oldest building was constructed around this time by another Huguenot, Paulus Regrenier, who built the first portion of the Manee House, still standing in disrepair at 509 Seguine Avenue.[161]

Over time, Old Town's original settlers also began to leave—in a literal sense—for the greener pastures of other parts of the island. Pierre Billiou moved to the Great Kills area by 1675,[162] and a contemporary account noted that a New Town, or Nieuwe Dorp, had surpassed its population. The journal of Jaspar Dankers also recorded the state of Old Town in 1679: "There were seven houses, but only three in which any body lived. The others were abandoned, and their owners had gone to live on better places on the island, because the ground around this village was worn out and barren, and also too limited for their use."[163]

Nonetheless, the island community had grown significantly enough that by 1663, its residents were requesting a religious minister who could speak both French and Dutch. Stuyvesant chose the Reverend Samuel Drisius, who, years earlier, had been sent to New Netherland by the Classis of Amsterdam, the governing body of the Dutch Reformed Church, to begin preaching at Old Town once every other month.[164] The celebrant of the first formal religious service on Staten Island was sixty-three when

The Voorlezer's house at Historic Richmondtown is not as old as once believed. New research indicates that it was built in the mid-1700s rather than the original belief of 1696. *Library of Congress.*

he began making the dangerous crossing across the bay, but he managed to keep up the practice for eight years before his old age and failing health prevented him.[165]

It would be another decade of sharing preachers with neighboring jurisdictions before the Reverend Petrus Tesschenmacker took the helm as Staten Island's first resident Dutch Reformed minister. His tenure in the borough was short-lived, just two years, as was his life after taking his next position in Schenectady. In February 1690, "he and most of his church members were surprised by a band of French and Indians, and all were massacred. The *Dominie's* [pastor's] head was split open and his body burned up to the shoulders."[166]

Back on Staten Island, the first establishment of a formal congregation occurred in 1693.[167] Two years later, a survey of congregations in the colony by the English chaplain John Miller records that the Reverend David Bonrepos, a pastor who had previously helped found the first Huguenot church in New Rochelle,[168] was preaching to forty English, forty-four Dutch and thirty-six French families in a "meeting house."[169] Despite their different religious affiliations, Anglicans, Dutch Reformed congregants and others who did not have their own preacher prayed together for many years at this site, which was likely along the present Arthur Kill Road between Richmond Avenue and Giffords Lane.[170]

RULE, BRITANNIA!

The town leaders of Oude Dorp were not about to take chances in the earliest days, regardless of whether the threats came from the natives or the menacing English to the east. The town was initially outfitted with six soldiers and six pounds of gunpowder to ward off any attacks during the initial settlement, of which, thankfully, none occurred.[171] In 1664, Stuyvesant reported back to the West India Company that its directives to establish fortifications near the Narrows had been undertaken in earnest. He described the wooden blockhouse on Staten Island as eighteen by twenty feet located in the center of the town's houses[172] and "provided with two or three light pieces of ordnance, of which one or two are *pedereroes*," a type of cannon capable of firing stone projectiles.[173]

The defenses and garrison proved inadequate, however, and Stuyvesant may have been exaggerating their strength to his bosses back home. On a

On September 8, 1664, Peter Stuyvesant heeded the pleas of New Amsterdam's leaders and clergy and signed the Articles of Capitulation, handing New Netherland to the English. *Library of Congress.*

hot August morning in 1664, they proved no match for an invading English force and may not have even fired a shot.

Days earlier, four menacing ships, the *Elias*, the *Martin*, the *William and Nicholas* and the flagship *Guinea*, had approached from Sandy Hook and dropped anchor across the Narrows in Gravesend Bay with thirty-six guns. These forces, including three companies of British troops, were under the command of Colonel Richard Nicolls, captain of the Duke of York's garrison at Portsmouth, and who was soon to be named deputy governor of the conquered colony.[174]

For more than a week, the ships waited at their anchorage off Coney Island while Nicolls ensured that he could get the cooperation and, of course, submission to the Crown from English settlers who had already begun to populate the sparse villages of Long Island. The main landing at Gravesend would not occur until August 25, but as a precursor to what would occur 120 years later during the Revolution, the British sent their first troops ashore to secure strategically critical Staten Island.[175]

On Thursday, August 18, 1664, a detachment of fifty men from Nicolls's company pushed off from the decks of the small flotilla and rowed across the calm summer waters of Lower New York Bay before setting aground on the shore of Staten Island near South Beach. They marched inland and up to the hamlet of Oude Dorp, where they found just "six decrepit old soldiers," who timidly surrendered control of the blockhouse. The entrance to the port of New Amsterdam was now effectively blockaded, thanks in part to the first landing of British regular troops in North America.[176] Dutch rule of Staten Island was over, and soon all of New Netherland would follow.

3

THE COUNTY OF RICHMOND, THE PROVINCE OF NEW YORK

In the summer of 1664, Peter Stuyvesant was not surprised when he received word of an English squadron sighted off Sandy Hook, nor was he stunned as he learned that its commanders had already made contact with their countrymen who had long pushed their settlements south onto Long Island from the Connecticut mainland. From the parapets of Fort Amsterdam, the director stood resolute in the face of the coming fight as he gazed out into the bay, hoping to hold the line against the most serious crisis to threaten the colony in its forty years. The men behind its ramparts looked down their gun barrels at the real-life manifestation of an invasion that they had likely imagined countless times before. The four approaching frigates tacked up the bay at full sail with their red-and-white ensign trailing proudly from their sterns.

The fleet's appearance was not a complete surprise, however, as the risk of a renewed Anglo-Dutch conflict had grown considerably since England's Stuart Restoration, a renewed hostile posture toward Holland.[177] Charles II, the third sovereign of the Stuart dynasty, had been restored to the monarchy in 1660, eleven years after the execution of his father, Charles I, during the English Civil War. His ascension and the subsequent stability of England allowed its leaders to look outward and ushered a return to protectionist policies designed to combat the economic and military threat from the Dutch overseas colonies.[178]

With a Stuart king firmly on the throne, Parliament passed its second Navigation Act in 1660, with the intention of hampering the West India

Company's ability to profit from the Americas. English colonial governors were also instructed to exploit any opportunity to harass their Dutch neighbors.[179] Furthermore, the Crown maintained that it held true title to all of the land on the Eastern Seaboard between Spanish Florida and French Canada. As a result, Charles II granted his brother, James, the Duke of York, all of the territory the Dutch claimed as part of New Netherland, including Staten and all of the other islands in the bay. It was York, yearning for an active role in renewed Anglo-Dutch hostilities, who would outfit the expedition that sailed into the harbor in 1664 to demand the peaceful surrender of Fort Amsterdam from Peter Stuyvesant.[180]

The Dutch colony was not entirely unprepared, and while Charles II and the Duke of York were putting together the pieces for the invasion, Stuyvesant and the Dutch government were busy taking what precautions they could. In 1661, as Stuyvesant tried to establish more settlements around the bay, the Dutch States-General issued a proclamation of "conditions and privileges" to advertise New Netherland's agricultural abundance and religious tolerance to the Puritans of New England or any other potential new colonists from the British Isles.[181] Stuyvesant had corresponded with neighboring New England governors and made a journey to Boston in 1663, hoping that the Puritans, who were generally against the restoration of the monarchy, might join a new cooperation between the colonies instead of falling in with the Crown's invasion force. His mission to New England was unsuccessful in its overall purpose, but it did manage to bear a critical fruit. A confidant Stuyvesant met while in Massachusetts would soon send him a note to warn of the impending invasion after Nicolls's squadron landed at Boston for supplies and colonial recruits.[182]

The director also tried to appease the interloping New England settlers on eastern Long Island with the offer of a truce. He estimated that they could muster "170 to 180 men, foot, and horse"[183] and feared that from there they could easily plunder Dutch settlements farther west and even threaten Fort Amsterdam itself. Again, these entreaties met with failure as Connecticut's governor John Winthrop declared that all of Long Island was no longer subject to New Netherland's rule.[184]

All of these fears came to fruition on August 30, 1664, when Nicolls sent a formal demand for the surrender of Fort Amsterdam. From atop the fort's walls, Stuyvesant could see not only more than one hundred guns of the English fleet trained on his meager force but also twice his number of soldiers and mounted militia from Connecticut and eastern Long Island amassed along the opposite bank of the East River. They were preparing to cross just below the village of Breuckelen.[185]

For a week, the standoff ensued, and day after day Stuyvesant was urged to surrender—first from Nicolls, who guaranteed "every man in his Estate, life, and liberty."[186] Governor Winthrop followed with the next plea, and then finally it began to come from New Amsterdam's own citizens and clergy. With seemingly no other option and with the high prospect of reasonable terms for Dutch colonists, the director appointed a commission that included Staten Island's Johannes de Decker to negotiate the terms.

On Monday, September 8, 1664, Stuyvesant and the commissioners signed the Articles of Capitulation and led their men out of the fort with full military honors. Six columns of British and New England troops marched into the city on parade past the assembled government of New Netherland and its citizens, with colors flying and drums sounding loud tattoos.[187] The English flag was raised over Manhattan for the first time at the fort, renamed Fort James, as its 1,500 citizens[188] became subjects of Charles II and were placed under the immediate authority of the newly appointed Governor Nicolls. The sun had set on Dutch colonial endeavors in North America.

CHANGE COMES

As proprietor of the former Dutch holdings, James Stuart, Duke of York and future King of England, had nearly absolute power over the conditions and government of his new colony. That said, his treatment of former Dutch settlers was objectively kind, and neither he nor his colonial governor believed that punishing the inhabitants would amount to much good for the colony's bottom line.[189]

In 1665, Nicolls formally granted the residents of New Amsterdam the right to govern themselves according to the customs of England and sought to empower men who were well regarded by the colony's electorate. As a result, Thomas Willett, an English resident for many years and an ally of Stuyvesant, became the first mayor of the city under English rule, while Manhattan's former *schout* (the second-highest Dutch position) became its first sheriff.[190]

On Staten Island, where Pierre Billiou had emerged as the settlement's leading man, that pattern played out differently. Previously, Billiou had been elected to serve as one of the town's two representatives at an assembly of Dutch colonists at Flushing and served locally as the island's schout. But when the English took over the island, they did not look to Dutch Loyalists like him to maintain control and were suspicious of the more open hostility he and other Dutch Protestants on the island had to English rule.[191]

Interestingly, the suspicions over Billiou's loyalty would be confirmed during the brief period in 1673–74 when the Dutch recaptured control of New York. He was once again appointed schout and seems to have been zealous in his efforts to restore the West India Company's authority, illegally seizing firearms held by an English-aligned neighbor. Eventually, when the English retook the colony, he was forced to return the guns.[192]

Instead of Billiou, the English sought a relative outsider to lead Staten Island. In September 1667, Nicolls granted Nicholas Stillwell a plantation, allowing him to be elected as its first sheriff. In this post, he could appoint deputies and was empowered with the authority to "decide and determine all matters of debt and difference."[193]

Stillwell was born around 1610 in Surrey, England, and first immigrated to the colony of Virginia before making his way north as one of the first settlers of Gravesend in 1646. Once in New Netherland, he was loyal to the Dutch and served as a lieutenant in the militia during a sporadic war against the Esopus Indians of the Hudson Valley between 1659 and 1663.[194] It was his veritable Dutch credentials and his English pedigree that likely made him Nicolls's preferred choice to govern a growing hamlet with a population as diverse as New Amsterdam.

The estate he was awarded was in the town of Dover, a name he may have bestowed on it himself, as the line of hills on Staten Island that face approaching ships could have reminded him of the fabled cliffs of his home in southeast England. In all likelihood, it was just the name the English gave to Old Town,[195] and the fact that Stillwell's son became the second inhabitant of the Billiou-Stillwell-Perine house in that neighborhood is evidence of that scenario.[196]

Of course, Dover was not the only name to be changed by the English. Almost as soon as the West India Company's colors were struck, Nicolls proclaimed that Fort Orange would be renamed Albany after his patron James's Scottish ducal title, while both New Amsterdam and the entirety of New Netherland would be known as New York.[197]

In the last decades of the seventeenth century, the English would also make changes to the structure of Staten Island's government and its role in relation to New York City and the broader province. Shortly after the

The Billiou-Stillwell-Perine house has stood in its original spot on Richmond Road in Dongan Hills for over 350 years and was the seventeenth-century home of two important Staten Island families. *New York Public Library.*

conquest, Nicolls reconstituted the southern portion of New York, including Westchester, Long Island and Staten Island, into a new shire called Yorkshire. This was further subdivided into three "ridings" for the purpose of establishing courts and levying taxes. In this, Staten Island was grouped with the small collection of towns in present-day Brooklyn in the West Riding. The government of Yorkshire initially consisted of a high sheriff, a lesser sheriff, constables and justices of the peace for each riding, all serving at the de facto pleasure of the governor.[198] Interestingly, New York City was excluded from the shire system and was given the privilege of establishing its own elected government "known and called by the Name & Style of Mayor Alderman & Sherriff, according to the Custom of England in his other Majesties Corporations."[199]

For a decade, Staten Island's legal cases were heard three times per year at the Court of Sessions for the West Riding at Gravesend.[200] However, in October 1675, the colonial government awarded it greater autonomy, declaring, "That by reason of Separation by Water Staten Island shall have a Jurisdiction of itself; and to have no further dependence on the Courts of Long Island, nor on their Militia."[201] From this point on, it would have its own separate judicial district. This lasted for almost 225 years, until the borough was consolidated into New York City in 1898.

The records of these court proceedings, the oldest of which are from 1680, were filed with the first clerk of Staten Island, Obediah Holmes, and have been maintained by the county clerk's office for over 335 years.[202] Although the ink on the pages is faded and worn, they paint a picture of the trials and tribulations of life on colonial Staten Island. In addition to recording deeds and cattle marks, the records also tell the stories of the conflicts and capers that undoubtedly created the gossip of the day. There was Thomas Walton's 1680 case against William Britten after the defendant's "unruly horses" broke a fence and destroyed crops.[203] Then in 1681, Aran Johnson allegedly set dogs on the pigs of one of his neighbors, for which he was given the choice of paying a fine or killing his dogs.[204]

Yet, the most interesting case among these records may be that of Mary Uselton. In January 1681, two witnesses testified that the unmarried and pregnant Ms. Uselton was unable to name the baby's father because, in her own words, "more than twenty men had laid with me." Just three months later, the mystery may have been solved, and perhaps the promiscuous Staten Islander lived out her days in happiness, when a widower named Jacob Cornelius married her and amended his will to share his estate "among all my children."[205]

THE MOST SIGNIFICANT CHANGE with respect to the self-governance of Staten Island came in 1683, when Thomas Dongan assumed the governorship of New York. In that year, the Duke of York allowed the inhabitants of his colony to form a provincial assembly, something that had long been promised. The duke would retain the right to appoint the governor but conceded direct elections and extensive lawmaking ability to the new legislature, which went well beyond the authority granted to other English colonies by the king.[206] In 1685, when James succeeded as king after the death of his brother, he would actually renege on the assembly, and it would not reconvene until 1691.[207]

Nonetheless, in 1683, Dongan issued edicts authorizing elections on Staten Island and elsewhere, and the delegates took their seats on October 17. Their first act, which is unsurprising when one considers that most of the representatives were Dutch, was to provide religious freedoms to all residents of the colony and implement a degree of taxation by consent. The second piece of legislation was to change how New York was

Richmond County gets its name from Charles Lennox, Duke of Richmond (1672–1723), the illegitimate son of King Charles II. *Yale Center for British Art.*

subdivided, forming the city of New York and the twelve original counties of the province of New York.[208] These county lines would remain largely unchanged until the city's consolidation in 1898. This, of course, included the provision for Staten Island: "The County of Richmond to contain all Staten Island, Shooters Island and the Islands of Meadow on the Westside thereof."[209] For the first time, two hundred families of the new County of Richmond were granted permanent seats in the new assembly and assessed a county tax of fifteen pounds. The name was derived from the king's illegitimate son the Duke of Richmond.[210]

The county would be further divided into political subdivisions over the next several decades, and one of the earliest references to this comes from a 1713 act of the assembly allowing the election of surveyors for "laying out and regulating the High-ways within the several divisions in said County of Richmond."[211] By the mid-1700s, four separate towns would be clearly defined, each with its own supervisor, named Castleton, Northfield, Southfield and Westfield. Additionally, the tax records show the county levies were divvied up four ways,[212] and after the Revolution, the four townships were once again defined by the New York State legislature on March 7, 1788.[213]

A GROWING ISLAND

Once installed as governor, Richard Nicolls turned some of his attention to settling Staten Island with new English colonists. In 1668, seeing good soil and a sparse population, he used land in the county to reward four of his soldiers who had served since the invasion. Henry Hedger, Thomas Walton, Nicholas Doddiman and John Kingdom all received large tracts of land near Old Town, between the shoreline and present-day Fingerboard Road and Sand Lane. These would be some of his final actions as governor, as later that year, the duke replaced him with Colonel Francis Lovelace.[214]

Lovelace's tenure would prove significant to the development of Staten Island, since it was during his term that Lenape title to the island was definitively extinguished. The danger from native attacks didn't subside after the English conquest, and when tensions arose in 1669, the new governor commissioned Pierre Billiou to raise a company of militia to guard residents and property. But desperate for a lasting peace, he also ordered Richard Stillwell and others to begin talks for a new deal with Raritan elders.[215]

The formal negotiations with the Raritan sachems began on April 7, 1670, inside Fort James, which is coincidentally now the site of the Old Customs House and National Museum of the American Indian. The Lenape had undoubtedly learned a great deal about negotiating with Europeans by then, and the price they received for Staten Island was well above what the English originally offered and significantly higher than the legendary price of Manhattan. They came prepared, and when they met with Governor Lovelace, Mayor Cornelius Steenwyck and Council Secretary Matthias Nicolls (Richard's nephew), they were armed with the maps and paperwork needed to negate some of the original Dutch and English patents. For several days the parties deliberated, and on April 13, a deal was struck, payment exchanged and documents signed. On May 2, 1670, Thomas Lovelace, the governor's brother, and Matthias Nicolls were appointed to take official possession of Staten Island on behalf of the duke in a formal ceremony of surrender.[216]

Recent research on the 1670 deed, by Andrew Lipman of Barnard College, shed new light on the circumstances surrounding its signers. The document, which is housed in the archives of the New York Historical Society, notably contains the signatures of ten younger individuals. In addition to the marks of the governor, mayor and eight members of the council, signatures for William Nicolls, Humphrey Devenport, Cornelis Bedloo and Nicholaes Antony were noted separately as "4 youths."[217] Additionally, the document was amended on April 15 to add the marks of six Native American children, three girls and three boys ranging from five to twenty years old, who signed the document in the presence of Governor Lovelace.[218] No minutes exist to indicate why children were asked to witness such a momentous document. However, Lipman believes the practice of requiring the next generation to sign important settlements had precedent in colonial negotiations with various indigenous peoples, who hoped that the agreement would last long after those who brokered it passed on. The permanence of the deed was clearly a concern, as it stipulated that it was to be renewed by both parties in person each year.[219]

Almost immediately after taking title, Lovelace was eager to open Richmond County to expanded settlement, but his initial plans fell short of the mark. At the end of 1669, he wrote to the governor of Bermuda to make an offer to his own colonists to incorporate a new town on the southwest portion of Staten Island, where "there was want of nothing."[220] He offered acres of "ploughable or arable land," low taxes and "liberty to elect and choose their own minister."[221] However, none of these seemed to entice any immigrants from the warmer island.

Lovelace's next attempt was better planned. In October 1670, the governor gave Captain Jacques Cortelyou orders to survey the island and subdivide it into two towns with forty families each. Although he didn't name it, the first town was likely the existing Old Town, as he ordered Cortelyou to add twenty-two lots to the eighteen that had already been settled by that time. For the second, consisting of forty new lots, he commanded him to "go to ye great kill and pitch up ye most convenient place for a towne."[222]

Cortelyou was the right man for the job. In addition to being one of the successful founders of New Utrecht a decade earlier, he served both the Dutch and English governments as its chief surveyor, laying out New Amsterdam's second official town map in 1660.[223]

His speculative work on Staten Island was not for naught, as there was interest in the properties before his survey was even completed. The council minutes of January 25, 1671, record Governor Lovelace as even boasting that several "application[s] hath been made unto me by diverse persons since my Resolution of ye settlement of ye New Townes."[224]

Soon the lots were granted to many Huguenot and English settlers, including Guyon's patent in Oakwood and to the governor's own brother Captain Dudley Lovelace, who received a substantial 150 acres. Many modern street names are linked with those who came in this wave, including Comely, Watson, Martineau and Britton.[225] Additionally, Abraham Lakeman was granted land in New Dorp in 1675, and his son built their family home on the property about five years later. The Lakeman House, which now stands at 2286 Richmond Road and is part of a thriving florist business, remains the oldest non-landmarked building in the borough.[226]

Governor Lovelace took personal and earnest efforts to grow his "Two Townes" on Staten Island. Three years after Cortelyou's survey, the New York government was advertising in Europe under one of his successors, Governor Edmund Andros, offering sixty acres of Richmond County for every freeman, fifty for wives and children and another fifty for indentured servants "after the expiration of their services according to ye customs of the country."[227]

These recruitment efforts proved successful, as the population swelled well beyond the initial dozen or so families who founded Old Town. By 1679, over one hundred separate land patents had been granted to new Staten Islanders, most of these having been surveyed, plotted and mapped by Robert Ryder in 1676. One of the largest grants of the period was for 422 acres of the North Shore to John Palmer, who was given riparian rights to Clove Brook and allowed to construct one of the island's first mills.[228] The property included much of what would now be considered West New Brighton and Port Richmond, including the area around Palmer Avenue.[229] Also patented at this time was the area then called Norwood, which consisted of the estate granted to Andrew Norwood in modern Clifton and Stapleton, where Norwood Avenue now runs. Other names on Ryder's map included "Shooters Island," after the small island where the Dutch enjoyed hunting geese; "ye Old Towne," near its present location; and "Lovelace," an early name for St. George and not anywhere near present-day Lovelace Avenue in Arden Heights.[230]

The most complete account of the island's progress in the late seventeenth century comes from the aforementioned journal of Jasper Dankers, who, along with his companion Peter Sluyter, traveled through Richmond County from June 11 to 13, 1679.[231] The following are selected excerpts from his diary:

> *11th, Wednesday—The woods are used for pasturing horses and cattle.... Game of all kinds is plenty, and twenty-five or thirty deer are sometimes seen in a herd.... We tasted here the best grapes....*
>
> *We went in to the first house* [in Old Town], *which was inhabited by English, and there rested ourselves and eat, and inquired further after the road; the woman was cross, and her husband not much better.... We proceeded by tolerably good road...* [and] *saw a house at a distance to which we directed ourselves across the bushes; it was the first house of the Niewe Dorp. We found there an Englishman who could speak Dutch, and who received us very cordially into his house, where we had as good as he and his wife had.*
>
> *12th, Thursday—The man where we slept set us on the road. We had no more villages to go to, but went from one plantation to another, for the most part belonging to the French.*
>
> *About one-third of the distance from the south side to the west end is still all woods, and is very little visited. We had to go along the shore* [likely from Eltingville south], *finding sometimes fine creeks well provided with wild turkeys, geese, snipes and wood hens....Proceeding thus along, we came to the west point* [Tottenville], *where an Englishman lived alone, some distance from the road. We ate something here, and he gave us the consolation that we would have a very bad road for the next two or three hours ahead* [heading north]*....There was a large creek to cross* [Mill Creek, Richmond Valley] *which ran very far into the land....After we had gone a piece of the way through the woods, we came through a valley with a brook running through it* [likely Charleston or Rossville]*....After continuing this course for about an hour, we saw at a distance a miserably constructed tabernacle of pieces of wood covered with*

brush, all open in front, and where we thought there were Indians, but on coming up to it we found in it an Englishman sick, and his wife and child lying upon some bushes by a little fire.... I never, in all my life, saw such poverty.... We went on, and had not gone far before we came to another house, and thus from one to another, French, Dutch and a Few English [likely Huguenot, Arden Heights, then Greenridge].

13th, Friday—We pursued our journey this morning, from plantation to plantation, the same as yesterday, until we came to that of Pierre Gardinier, who had been in the service of the Prince of Orange, and had known him well. He had a large family of children and grand-children. He was about seventy years of age, and was still as fresh and active as a young person. After we had breakfasted here, they told us that we had another large creek to pass called the Fresh Kill, and then we could set across the Kill Van Kull to [Elizabethtown], *where we might wait for a boat to the Manhattans.*[232]

THE MANOR AT BENTLEY

The "Englishman who lived alone" who Dankers and Sluyter shared a meal with at the western terminus of Staten Island on June 12 was Christopher Billopp and would be the progenitor of the most important families in the story of Richmond County for the next one hundred years.

The Billopp family came from Coventry, England. Christopher was the great-grandson of Barnard Billopp, a sixteenth-century cavalryman who died in a duel with a fellow officer. His grandfather James was a friend of Elizabeth I, and his father, Christopher, was a government contractor held in high regard by Charles I. Through the patronage of the king, Christopher Sr. sent his only son to naval college, and he soon found adventures on the high seas as an English captain.[233]

How Billopp came to possess a large estate styled the Manor of Bentley at the tip of Staten Island and the southernmost corner of New York is the plot of two stories, one of which is grounded in documentary evidence and the other steeped in legend. Neither is exclusive of the other.

First, the more factual account. The "bold spirited sea-roving Captain of the British navy with influence at court" came to the province of New York in command of a company of soldiers with Governor Andros in 1674.[234] A year earlier, hostilities had once again broken out between

Christopher Billopp's grand estate house at the Manor of Bentley, built around 1680, is more commonly known to Staten Islanders as the Conference House. *Library of Congress.*

England and Holland, and a Dutch fleet of nineteen ships and six hundred men under Anthony Colve sailed into New York Bay. With the assistance of loyal Dutch colonists, including some Staten Islanders, like Pierre Billiou, they managed to wrestle control back from the English for what would prove to be a short-lived takeover. The Treaty of Westminster, in February 1674, nullified the conquest,[235] but Billopp and his company were sent to North America to put pressure on the Dutch during the negotiations.[236] The following year, the reward for his service was granted, and the Provincial Council estimated that "the Neck of Land Capt. Billopp is upon, is judged to be about 1,300 acres,"[237] despite the fact that the actual patent he received from Andros on March 25, 1676, judged it at only 1,000.[238]

Over the next decade, Billopp's career would see highs and lows. In 1677, he was appointed commander and collector of customs in the Delaware watershed, but by 1679, he was recalled by Andros to account for having "misconducted" himself.[239] Once back on Staten Island, he was involved in numerous lawsuits and disputes with his neighbors. Still, the stories of his behavior did not cause him to fall out of favor with the Stuart court or the governor of New York, and in 1687, the council created the Lordship or Manor of Bentley and enlarged his estate to 1,600 acres.[240]

Why Billopp was granted such a large patent is the subject of conjecture. Most likely, it was the result of his father's influence at court or his prior success in the navy. But as folklore would tell it, the second version of events centered on a legendary feat of local seamanship.

That story of how Billopp came to own the Manor of Bentley began in 1664, when the then Duke of York bestowed the future land of New Jersey to Lord John Berkeley and Sir George Carteret.[241] The grant gave them all lands "lying westward of Long Island, and [Manhattan] Island, and bounded on the east part by the main sea, and part by Hudson's River."[242] From the text, it would seem that Staten Island is, in all likelihood, part of the New Jersey patent, as the path of the Hudson would normally be considered to exit the bay through the Narrows. Yet, it was clear that the Duke wasn't willing to part with Richmond so soon.

In 1668, the duke is said to have declared that any island in the Hudson estuary that could be circumnavigated in twenty-four hours would be considered part of New York. Whether Staten Island could be circled in a day had long been a subject of friendly debates and dares among the locals, but it was the newly landed Captain Billopp who accepted the challenge. According to the tale, he loaded the decks of his small ship, *Bentley*, with empty barrels, giving him just the right ballast against the wind. Once in the shallow waters of the Arthur Kill, he cast them overboard as makeshift buoys to ride high in the water and over the sandbars. He finished with an hour to spare.[243]

Whether this story is true is a matter of folklore, and the question of Staten Island's provenance was the cause of continued uncertainty. At no time was it ever a part of New Jersey, despite its proprietors' best efforts. In 1672, Governor Carteret attempted to cut hay on Staten Island, triggering the first of many legal border disputes, and similar infringements followed in 1675, 1681, 1684 and 1704.[244] The issue would not truly be put to rest until 1833.

For Christopher Billopp, his circumnavigation of the island was not to be his final escapade. In his remaining life, he alternated between England and his estate, constantly working with his father's contacts at court to remain in good standing. In 1693, he was charged with the crime of "kicking and beating" a Staten Islander named William Bryan, but no penalty was recorded.[245] He had likely also resumed a successful life in the navy. The *Biographia Navalis*, a record of Britain's naval officers, lists a Captain Christopher Billopp as commanding the ninety-gun *Ossory* in 1692. Less than a year later, he was promoted to the *Victory* and then the *London*, both first-rate ships of the line.[246]

It is unclear whether or not he returned to the Manor of Bentley later in life, as his will was made in England on April 25, 1724, as he was held in fleet prison. He passed away a year later.[247] By 1702, his daughter Anne and her husband, Thomas Farmar, who served as the mayor of New Brunswick and a New Jersey state assemblyman, had become the principal residents of the manor. To satisfy the desires of her father, their third son, Thomas, who next inherited the estate, took the name Billopp, and the family surname continued on Staten Island for several generations.[248]

The Manor of Bentley's longest-lasting legacy would be the rubble stone colonial–style Conference House, which still stands in the city park of the same name and is called that in honor of a failed 1776 Staten Island peace conference in advance of the British invasion of Manhattan. The home was first built by Captain Billopp around 1680 and was owned by his family until the conclusion of the Revolution, when it was confiscated without compensation by the new government.

Dongan and His Hills

In 1683, New York was blessed with a new governor. By both contemporary and historical accounts, Thomas Dongan is seen as one of the most highly regarded colonial politicians. He was a man who was "fitted to inspire confidence to all around him,"[249] and his influence on the development of the province and of its southernmost county cannot be overstated.

Dongan was a scion of the Irish Catholic nobility, and his father was a Loyalist member of the Irish Parliament. His brother was the First Earl of Limerick, a title he accidentally inherited in 1698 after his nephew's untimely death by cannonball while serving James II at the Battle of the Boyne.[250] Thomas Dongan also served the Crown as a colonel in an Irish regiment of English Loyalists during the Commonwealth period, while he and his family lived in exile in France. In that time, he befriended the future king and gained his confidence, leading to his appointment as governor of his growing colony despite his problematic Catholicism.[251]

Dongan is perhaps most notable for giving New York its shape, as it was he who pushed back against French incursions from the north and held the line along the St. Lawrence and the Great Lakes.[252] It was also Governor Dongan who ordered an election and presided over the first meeting of the Provincial Assembly, which established the province's charter of Liberties

Thomas Dongan, Second Earl of Limerick (1634–1715), was appointed governor of the province of New York in 1683 and was granted an estate on Staten Island, which he named Castletowne after his birthplace in Ireland. *New York Public Library.*

and Privileges and chartered its twelve original counties, including Richmond.[253]

On Staten Island, the neighborhood of Dongan Hills is named in his honor, despite his actually not settling in that part of the county. In fact, his property in that area was limited.

In 1687, over five thousand acres along the Kill Van Kull were surveyed and established as the "the Lordshippe and mannor of Cassiltowne,"[254] a name derived from Dongan's ancestral seat in County Kildare, and one that still designates the neighborhood. The governor enjoyed his Richmond County properties. He spent much time there after his retirement, and while in office, he was noted for missing council meetings while "engaged at his hunting lodge on Staten Island killing bears." Interestingly, the beasts of Staten Island were quite a problem during the Dongan administration, and one of the earliest laws his Provincial Assembly passed was to mandate that a twenty-shilling "reward be given for Killing of Wolves on Staten Island."[255]

The bulk of the governor's aggression was not spent on wild game, however, as he had to contend with attacks from the French and their native allies along his northern and western frontiers. By 1687, this occupied nearly all of his attention and forced him to take up full-time residence in Albany, leaving New York City in the hands of a lieutenant.

Although the conflict was far from the province's southernmost county, Staten Island had a role to play. Thomas Stillwell was ordered to organize the militia, and in 1689, its officers were listed as Jacques Poillon and Cornelis Corsen, captains of foot; Lieutenants Thomas Morgan and John Van Pelt; and Ensigns Seger Gerritsen and Cornelis Nevius.[256]

Richmond County was also required to burden its share of the war costs. The taxes, at first, were relatively small, but over time they grew proportionally with the escalating conflict.[257] In May 1691, the county was assessed £120 for its share in supporting the annual cost of one hundred fusiliers in Albany.[258] By September, an additional £90 was needed as "the Frontiers at Albany [were] in Eminent danger to be lost, being daily threatened to be invaded by the French."[259] In the following spring, another £67 was required.[260]

Governor Dongan was not above bearing the personal costs to outfit his northern expeditions. In 1689, desperate for cash, he mortgaged his lands in the colony for five years to Robert Livingston, including all of Castletown and other holdings near Old Town, as well as large tracts in the Hudson Valley, Queens and on Martha's Vineyard. In total, this raised £2,172. His debt must have been satisfied, as the Manor of Castletown and his other Richmond County properties were bequeathed to his nephews, Thomas, John and Walter, in 1715, just before his death.[261]

The true test of Dongan's abilities as governor did not arise from events in the damp forests of western New York but rather much farther away in the height of luxury and decadence at the Château de Fontainebleau, where the "Sun King" Louis XIV revoked the Edict of Nantes in 1685. The persecution of France's Protestants, as earlier mentioned, led to a significant emigration of Huguenots. Yet even before this seminal event, France had begun a system of coercion and intimidation know as Les Dragonnades in which companies of poorly behaved dragoons were billeted among Protestants households, eating, taking and destroying what they could until the owner of the home rejoined the Roman Catholic faith. In just the first few months, thirty-five thousand converted, while many more fled.[262]

In New York, and especially on Staten Island where there was a diverse group of Protestants, tensions ran high as to how, when and if religious oppression might rear its head. England was, after all, a Protestant country whose king was expected to protect its Protestant citizens. However, James II was a Roman Catholic, as were the majority of the officers of his army. Furthermore, the most important leaders of New York were also Catholic, including Governor Dongan, Lieutenant Governor Brockholls and Major Baxter, the commander of the provincial forces defending Albany.[263]

The king sensed the unease and sought to mitigate it by consolidating all of England's northeastern colonies under one administration. For this, he returned the Protestant Edmund Andros to power and appointed a Protestant lieutenant governor to replace Dongan in direct control of New York.[264] Despite the precautions in the colonies and at home, England descended into the turmoil known as the Glorious Revolution, when William of Orange and his wife, Mary, James's Protestant daughter, crossed the channel and deposed King James II to install themselves as coregents.

In the colonies, fear led to rumors of a Catholic takeover in an effort to restore the government of James II. This echoed well beyond the borders of New York, and in the summer of 1689, Maryland's non-Catholics joined forces to overthrow the provincial government of the Lords Baltimore.[265] At the same time, Jacob Leisler, a prominent German merchant and member of the council, effectively seized control of the city of New York, calling Dongan, Nicholson and colonial government "a pack of rogues and papists."[266]

Fearing a Catholic counterplot, colonists of all faiths throughout the province were ordered disarmed. For Dongan, New York's most prominent Catholic, and one who formerly paid "Romish priests"[267] from the public purse, it was impossible to remain safe in obscure retirement, even at his estate at Cassiltowne. In 1690, a warrant for his arrest was issued, and he was forced to flee from his homes, first on Long Island, then Staten Island, New Jersey and finally on to Boston.[268]

Dongan may not have been entirely innocent, either. His brigantine (a small two-masted ship) anchored off Staten Island was outfitted with cannons, and the commander of the ship refused the Leisler government's attempts to search it. The excuse that it was outfitted to cross the Atlantic was plausible but not accepted. Further, as Bayles and other Staten Island

In 1689, Jacob Leisler (1640–1691) seized control of New York and declared that he and those signing his declaration would hold Fort James on behalf of William and Mary. *New York Public Library.*

chroniclers have claimed, several pieces of cannon were found hidden at Dongan's mill, which was just south of modern Post Avenue and could have been readied quickly.[269]

Throughout Leisler's rebellion, Richmond County remained in a tense state of unease as many of its citizens were Huguenots and Walloons who had already fled European persecution. With rumors running their course, their fears were not entirely unwarranted, as a real threat existed from French forces pushing south from Canada. Soon, the apprehensions turned to full panic, and Protestant families were documented to have constructed makeshift hiding places in the woods or slept in their boats anchored just offshore. Leisler disbanded the local authorities and replaced them with men loyal to his cause who aggressively pursued and harassed any potential threats, ironically trying to calm the county's nerves.[270] On December 19, 1689, he appointed Cornelis Corsen as captain and Cornelis Nevius as ensign of an infantry company that was to serve as the island's garrison.[271] In addition, the surviving Leisler papers record several Staten Islanders as soldiers who were sent north to meet any potential French Catholic incursion. These included Henrick Hendriksz, Jean Faere, Jean Marlett, Francis Mauriss and Jean Doulier.[272]

In March 1691, England sent a new force to retake possession of the colony under a newly appointed governor, Henry Slaughter. Leisler soon gave up and was tried and executed on May 16. His ringleaders on Staten Island, by then also including John Theunison, John Peterson and Gerard Vechten, were made to account for the "Riotts and Tumults" by paying three pounds in restitution, all as the province was placed was back under formal control.[273]

Once secure under the Protestant regency of William and Mary, the colonial government felt safe demanding reparations for the economic costs of the rebellion, both from physical damage to property and as an economic result of those fleeing their farms. In each county, commissioners were appointed to hear the claims of the "many hurts injurys wrongs and Damages [that] were done onto their Magestyes good and faithful Subjects by those...that usurped power and Government."[274] Many more Staten Islanders were forced to pay reparations to their neighbors as this rebellious chapter of provincial New York history came to a close.

THE ISLAND'S FAITHFUL

Around the turn of the eighteenth century, the only formal church to speak of on Staten Island was the French Church, where Reverend Bonrepos received land in Greenridge in 1698. It satisfied the ecclesiastical needs of the county's French, Dutch and English worshippers. Dutch settlers also had the option of attending the informal services of the Voorlezer. However, after some time, the number of congregants had grown to the point that a separate Dutch Reformed church was warranted.

Baptismal records for Staten Island's first Dutch Reformed church date to the 1696 birth of Marritie, the daughter of Jan Van Pelt.[275] For twenty years, there was no indication that the church had its own building; however, there is evidence to show that the services for a separate Dutch congregation on the North Shore had started as early as the 1680s. This early church was ministered through a series of visiting preachers, including the ill-fated Reverend Tessenmacker[276] and the Reverend Wiliam Bertholf, who was the pastor of congregations in Hackensack and Bergen and would ferry over for services.[277]

In 1680, there were only five homes in the area now known as Port Richmond, but by 1704, a description by road surveyors noted a well-populated cemetery in the area, indicating the town had grown significantly.[278] In 1715, Governor Richard Hunter formally gave representatives of the Reformed Protestant Dutch Church a grant to build a new church on "some convenient location" in that area.[279]

The cornerstone for the new Dutch Reformed church was laid in 1716, and construction of its hexagonal-shaped nave took over a year. By 1718, the new church had a pastor, Reverend Cornelius Van Santvoord, hailing from Leiden in South Holland. The congregants of Staten Island had appealed to the Classis of Amsterdam for a minister who could preach in Dutch and French, and it obliged by sending the young Van Santvoord, who remained pastor for twenty-four years.[280]

THE EARLY EIGHTEENTH CENTURY also saw the dawn of the Episcopal faith on Staten Island, with the formation of St. Andrew's Church, which still exists at its historic location.

In 1692, the devoutly religious Benjamin Fletcher was named governor of New York. He promptly set about to remedy what he felt was the colony's chief problem, that "Prophaneness and Liscentiousness

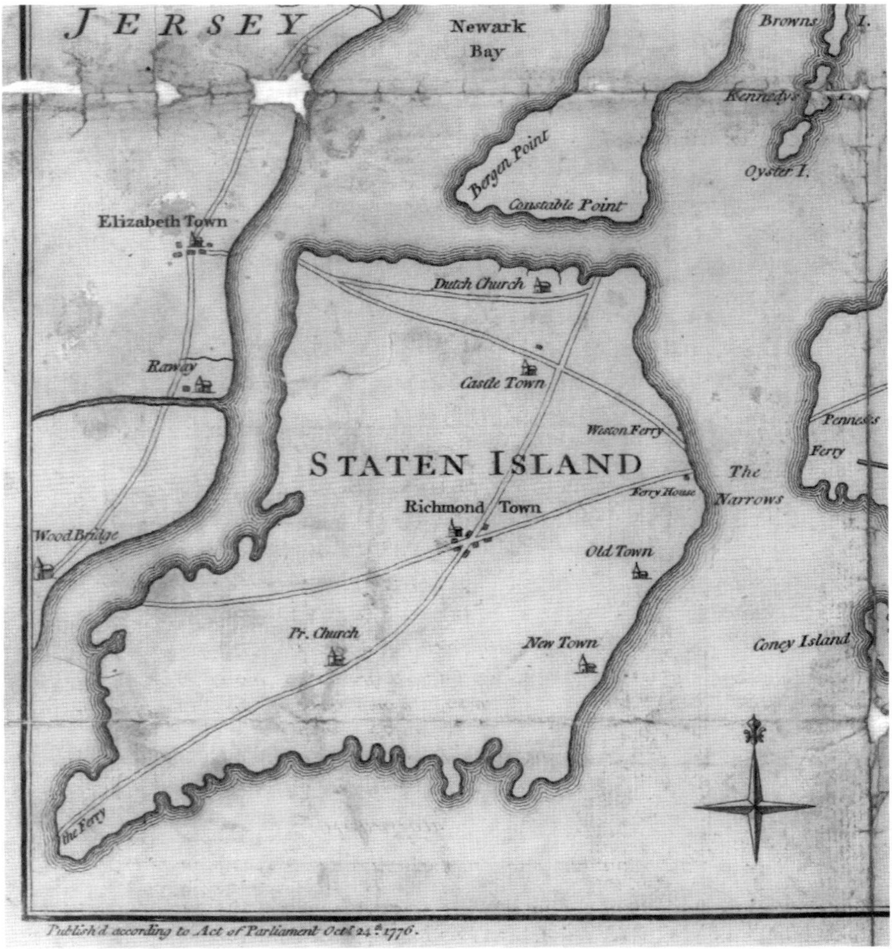

Detail of an eighteenth-century map showing the locations of the French Protestant church in Greenridge and the Dutch Protestant church in Port Richmond. *Library of Congress.*

hath of late over spread this Province for want of a settled Ministry."[281] His Ministry Act of 1693, which received the royal signature four years later, was a document that recalibrated New York's Episcopal Church and provided subsidies for ministers to preach on Staten Island and elsewhere around the harbor.[282] This act not only led to the founding of St. Andrew's on Staten Island but also of the famous Trinity Church on Broadway in Manhattan, which installed its first rector, William Vesey, on Christmas in 1697.[283]

On Staten Island, visiting preachers held regular Episcopal services in the town hall at Cockles Town (now Richmondtown) as early as 1702, by Reverends George Keith and John Talbot.[284] The two clergymen were missionaries sent by the Society of the Propagation of the Gospel in Foreign Parts, or the Venerable Society. After three years of growth, the county was finally granted its own pastor, Reverend Aeneas Mackenzie, also a Venerable Society missionary, and he remained its permanent vicar until his death in 1723.[285]

Mackenzie was consumed with the idea of building a new church on Staten Island. After a short time in his post, he outlined a proposal for a formal parish organization, which he named the Church of St. Andrew.[286] So enthralled in purpose was this Scottish preacher that when the Venerable Society offered to send him to serve as pastor of a potentially larger congregation in Stratford, Connecticut, doubling his salary, he rejected it, saying:

> *As to my being removed to Stratford though my encouragement might be considerably greater than where I am especially if the Society allow…£100 a year to a Missionary to that place as those of Stratford expect. Yet I could not in honor, as things now stand in my Parish desire to be removed for we are building of a Church in Staten Island which I hope will be under roof next September, and to leave those of Staten Island so after they have been at the trouble and charges of building a church for my encouragement to stay among them, would be a great discouragement to those of that Island in particular, and I humbly conceive of ill consequence to the church in general in these parts.*[287]

The parish was formally founded in 1708, and the cornerstone to the original St. Andrew's Church was laid in 1709. Construction continued for several years before its completion in the summer of 1712. In June of the following year, Queen Anne issued the official charter and sent two chalices and a paten as gifts[288] to the "decent and convenient Stone Church for the Service and Worship of God according to the Discipline of the Church of England."[289] The original structure was approximately twenty-five by forty feet but expanded over time. In 1718, a porch was added; in 1743, the nave was enlarged; and in 1774, it was again enlarged, and a steeple was built.[290]

Mackenzie's other great legacy to the church was the procurement of the Duxbury Glebe, which was critical to the church's prosperity until the

The original St. Andrew's Church was completed in about 1712 and survived the Revolution but was destroyed by two subsequent fires in 1867 and 1872. *Staten Island Historical Society.*

twentieth century. A glebe is a tract of land owned by a church and leased out or farmed to raise revenue for its support. The Duxbury Glebe was a farm of approximately 340 acres on the North Shore that was bequeathed in 1718 by one of the parish's elders and one of the early county clerks, Elias Duxbury. Its original boundaries were a large rectangle, now roughly from St. Peter's in New Brighton to Swan Street in Tompkinsville between St. Mark's Place and Monroe Avenue. The future governor Daniel Tompkins purchased 100 acres from the church in 1814, leading to the neighborhood of his name, and nineteenth-century real estate mogul Thomas E. Davis bought 94 acres to develop in 1834. By 1903, all of the church's landholdings were converted to investments, when the Duxbury Fund was valued at $84,150.[291]

A PEACEFUL AND PROSPEROUS HALF-CENTURY

At the turn of the eighteenth century, the Provincial Council began to place pressure on local county officials to conduct a census, likely with the goal of better organizing its methods of taxation. The calendar of council minutes mentions census orders five times between 1701 and 1703, including an order to take justices of the peace to task for neglecting to send in their reports.[292]

In 1706, Richmond County conducted its first census, reporting that there were 924 whites, with predominately Dutch and French names, and 127 blacks.[293] There is evidence that there were also still native Lenapes living on the island around this time, as their names are found sporadically through early baptismal records.[294] Additionally, we can deduce that a steady flow of Dutch and French colonists continued to immigrate to Richmond well into the eighteenth century from the registry of new cattle marks to dairy farmers found in the county court records.[295] At the time, nearly all Staten Islanders were farmers and identified themselves as "planters" in their wills. Many likely grew tobacco and corn, although dairy farming was the county's booming business.[296]

The eighteenth century was not dissimilar to modern times, and a growing population brought a new need for more infrastructure and organization. Richmond County's roads first received public attention in 1694, when Captain Billopp, then the appointed surveyor, was ordered by Governor Fletcher to lay out a series of roads.[297] The job was not fully carried out, however, and the order was reissued many times. There are numerous documents from this period recording Joseph Billopp (Captain Billopp's brother) and Jacques Poillon surveying and laying new roads, many of which still guide modern automobile drivers today.

In 1708, they formalized the path of the High Road to be "four rod broad" from the Watering Place in Tompkinsville to Captain Billopp's property in Tottenville.[298] This would become Van Duzer Street, Richmond Road and Amboy Road. In 1709, they laid out a "3 Rod, Broad English measure" road from the "head of the fresh Kill"[299] to the Billopp estate, which would eventually become Arthur Kill Road. Soon they would lay roads connecting Cockles Town to the North Shore, to new boat landings in Great Kills and to all of the mills and meetinghouses elsewhere and in between.[300] Over time, seven more acts to construct "Publick Highways" were passed before the Revolution.[301]

To get off the island, ferries were the only option, as no permanent bridges would be built until the late nineteenth century. There had long been service between the Watering Place and New York and from Tottenville to Amboy. In 1722, a new service was licensed to an Englishman, Anthony Wright, from Rossville to New Jersey, and in 1724, another one, to connect with Long Island, was granted to John Peters and Benjamin Bill. Later, direct service from Bay Ridge to the Clifton area by the Stillwell family would come in 1740, and new ferries from New York to the North and East Shores would open in 1747 and 1755, respectively.[302]

The education of the county's youth had also become a priority for colonial Staten Islanders. In addition to addressing their celestial needs, Reverend Mackenzie and the Venerable Society also sought to solve this worldlier problem by providing a fifteen-pound salary for two schoolmasters—an encumbrance they would bear straight through the Revolution. The students, some of whom were the children of slaves, were granted free tuition and given a rigorous religious curriculum through the use of prayer books and briefly, if ever, touching on secular topics.[303]

Despite any religious differences, it seems that there was little hesitation on the part of Staten Island parents in sending their kids to one of Mackenzie's classrooms. By 1711, he reported to the secretary of the Venerable Society that there were "two good schools upon the Island," and that "[t]he French, some of the Dutch, and what Dissenters we have excepting two of three Quaker families, allow their children to be taught the Church Catechism."[304]

Not all of these children grew up to be choir boys it would seem, as county officials had to also take measures to ensure law and order ruled the day. Around 1715, likely under the direction of Judge Thomas Farmar or Sheriff William Tillyer, a whipping post was erected at Cockles Town across the street from St. Andrew's Church along the rise of Richmond Hill.[305] A sharp bend around a since-removed nineteenth-century schoolhouse at the site gives the road its nickname of Snake Hill.[306]

Whipping had long been an accepted punishment in the colony. The initial English laws for New York allowed for lashing sentences for basic offences and even went much further for more serious crimes. For burglary, being "branded on the forehead" was warranted for the first offense, and the second time, one was "branded as before and severely whipped."[307]

Exactly how many times Staten Island's whipping post was used in the eighteenth century remains unclear. In *Morris's Memorial History of Staten Island*, which has proven to be less reliable than other sources, there is mention of two floggings in its first year. The first was a German colonist who refused to assist a constable in corralling a drunkard and the second was "a slave belonging to Mr. Ryerss" who allegedly entered the home of a Mr. DuPuy and stole property.[308]

The provincial government made other efforts to address the legal needs of Staten Islanders. In 1704, the Provincial Council authorized Richmond to assess its taxpayers to establish the first jail and government building on "such convenient place or places near the middle of said County."[309] This spot was almost certainly Cockles Town and was the beginning of Richmondtown's long history as the county seat. Whether construction problems were an issue or adequate financing was not in place, the council was forced to pass another resolution in 1719 for the same purpose.[310] Regardless of its problems, whatever early jail had actually been built by 1728 was "in Such a Condition that it is highly necessary to build a new one."[311] A larger and expanded courthouse would be constructed in the 1740s and lasted for many years.[312]

THE PRINCIPAL OCCUPATION OF Staten Islanders during this prosperous era was farming. Leading up to the Revolution, wheat became most the popular crop, while rye, barley, corn, tobacco and flax were also common. Near every farmhouse and hamlet, orchards of apples, cherries, peaches and pears could be found. Animals were critical to the economy as well. The island had no shortage of dairies and poultry farms, and Richmond's fattened cattle were sold at markets in the city and in New Jersey.[313]

Staten Island was also a source of manufactured and refined products. Licenses were granted to a number of mills along the island's inland waterways, with roads built to connect them. William Britton, for example, was licensed to construct a gristmill along Guyon's Creek in 1713,[314] likely on the site of the modern New York City wastewater plant still accessed by Mill Road. The Guyon family owned the creek and all of their property in the same neighborhood from their original grant in the late 1600s through the late 1800s,[315] when David Tysen began buying up large tracts.[316] All are recalled in the area's arterial street names. Other mills on the island ground various cereals, and given both the abundance of timber and the demand for wood in New York City, sawmills were also quite common.[317] Certain delicacies were also produced on Staten Island, as most homes had a smokehouse where hams, beef shoulders and various game meats could be cured.[318] Most cheerfully, by 1717, there were thirteen licenses granted in the county for "retailers of strong liquors."[319]

Staten Island was, at this time, a significant component of the provincial economy. Its situation at the mouth of the bay, along with its numerous inlets, ferries and road network, allowed its colonial producers to access the major markets of New York City. As the island's commercial fortunes blossomed, its residents began importing fine manufactured goods that were produced and shipped from Britain and its colonies. Unlike their neighbors in Westchester and on Long Island, Richmond's producers and merchants also had the option of exporting to New Jersey's three main ports—all just across the Kill at Elizabethtown, Woodbridge and Amboy. In fact, given the proximity and the regularity of ferry service, one can presume that Staten Island may have been economically dependent on its trade with New Jersey, while politically dependent on its leaders in New York City.[320]

As the island prospered, its populace grew. In the twenty years after its first census, the county's population doubled to nearly two thousand people.[321] Although its inhabitants lived in a sparse and scattered setting, even by eighteenth-century standards, Richmond County had a blossoming communal and social life. On Sundays, families would gather before and after their respective church services for activities and meals where they could interact with other members of their congregation and share gossip. On court days, the men from all over the county gathered at the county seat, where they would discuss the news of the day and the frustrations of their agricultural businesses. The most popular social occasions were reserved for the winter when, according to Richard Bayles, "those who were yet unmarried sought each other's society and met at Richmond to indulge in the merry dance until the waning hours admonished them to return to their homes."[322]

While the first half of the eighteenth century was, for the most part, peaceful for Staten Island, the specter of conflict and threats from native tribal warfare were never far off. The militia was an important institution and was called on numerous times in this period, and Richmond's taxpayers were routinely required to financially support its operations in the north. The 1711 muster roll lists nearly two hundred men in two companies, which at the time would have been about one-fifth of all residents.[323] No family seems to have been spared from serving.

The island itself was also prepared for potential conflicts. In 1703, £1,500 was allocated to construct a battery on both sides of the Narrows, and three years later, Richmond County was included in a broad provincial plan to fortify all of the approaches to the city.[324] This proposal may not have fully come to fruition because by 1711, the county was ordered to bear the cost of operating a signal beacon at the Narrows, consisting of "a great Gun with powder to charge, & Lighted Match to fire the same, & three of the Militia to be on duty day & night to watch."[325] Had a full battery been installed, a signal gun would not have been necessary.

Richmond's citizen-soldiers were not idle despite the general peace. The militia was mustered in 1704 when a French privateer attempting to impress sailors was sighted off Sandy Hook. It was mobilized again in expeditions against the French and Indians in Canada in 1711. The 1720s saw relative peace under Governor William Burnet, who was able to negotiate treaties with the northern tribes. However, hostilities resumed sporadically in 1740, 1752 and 1755. By 1758, the island's militia companies were on the march to Albany to participate in the first of two global conflicts that would shape the future of the colonial world.[326]

4
RICHMOND FRACTURES

The global conflict that became known as the Seven Years' War, engulfing Europe in massive mobilizations and hundreds of thousands of deaths, arguably began in 1754 with comparatively small skirmishes between British and French outpost garrisons in western New York and the Ohio Valley. The war's North American theater is commonly referred to as the French and Indian War, and its action centered on engagements between provincial and regular forces of Britain and France and their respective tribal allies. Fighting took place from Nova Scotia and the St. Lawrence in the north to the wilderness of modern West Virginia and the Great Lakes on the frontier. The province of New York saw much of the bloodshed, and Richmond's militiamen and the island itself played active roles.

After an initial stretch of French victories, the British turned to John Campbell, Earl of Loudoun, to command all forces. His job in 1756 and 1757 was to organize a proper military force out of the scattered remains of existing units on the continent—from new recruits and fresh regiments he had brought from Europe.[327] By this time, the province of New York had become the epicenter of the North American conflict and, along with New England, provided most of the colonial troops. It is not clear whether any Staten Islanders took part in the heavy fighting in this early stage of the war at Fort Oswego on Lake Erie or at Fort William Henry guarding Lake George. However, the overall British reliance on New York colonial troops caused headaches for Loudoun as he maneuvered his forces around the

Adirondacks. After spending as much time fighting with provincial officers as he did the French,[328] he was replaced.

In 1758, the British placed command of the army in new hands and assigned an even greater burden on counties like Richmond to produce both money and men. That April, Captain Thomas Arrowsmith raised a company of fifty-three enlistees on Staten Island. From the muster roll, it appears that the majority were of English descent, despite the still comparatively large population of French and Dutch speakers in the county.[329] This suggests that at this point, aiding in Britain's global and colonial goals may not have been a priority for many residents. Nonetheless, the men of Arrowsmith's company rendezvoused with the main body of New York's provincial regiment at Fort Edward in June 1758 and were placed under the command of Oliver De Lancey, the brother of New York's provincial governor, James De Lancey.[330]

The group's first action came soon after. Contemporary newspaper accounts place De Lancey's regiment among the eighteen thousand British soldiers ultimately under General James Abercrombie on July 8, 1758, who "form'd themselves in three Grand Divisions"[331] arrayed below the breastworks of the French-held Fort Ticonderoga. Situated on the left flank during a disastrous assault, the New York men were "surprised" by the French and withstood "the whole Fire of the Enemy for near an Hour."[332]

After the setback at Ticonderoga, Abercrombie, hoping to save face and capitalize on what he perceived to be the enemy's overextension, dispatched Lieutenant Colonel John Bradstreet and three thousand provincials to launch a surprise attack on Fort Frontenac at the mouth of the St. Lawrence Seaway. This force included a total of 1,112 New Yorkers[333] armed with twelve pieces of cannon and mortars, and the muster roll lists Arrowsmith's Richmond company among them.[334] The men traveled over four hundred miles in a matter of weeks, on land and in small boats, forcing the surrender of a small French garrison after just seven shells were fired.[335]

Staten Islanders likely remained engaged for the remainder of the conflict. The following season, Arrowsmith was able to raise forty-nine men with an enticing bounty of fifteen pounds,[336] and for the next four years, the island would become a vital part of the war effort.

Staten Island's position at the mouth of the Hudson made it a critical strategic position for Sir Jeffery Amherst, who would serve as the army's commander-in-chief for the final four years of the war. In 1761, he ordered three regiments of regular troops to make camp on Staten Island, including his own, the Fifteenth Regiment of Foot. He also sent the bloodied remnants

After his success against the French, Sir Jeffery Amherst (1717–1797) was awarded the Order of Bath (seen on his breastplate) in a ceremony on Staten Island in 1761. *Library of Congress.*

of the Royal Highlanders,[337] known as the Black Watch, who suffered 316 killed and over 300 wounded at Ticonderoga.[338]

In total, thousands of regiments encamped on the island in varying periods of time through June 1763, and Amherst used its shores and harbors as a staging area for major deployments throughout the Northeast and expeditions into the Caribbean.[339] The largest of these was the 1761 sortie to Martinique, of which the *New York Gazette* reported, "The troops that were encamped on Staten Island, consisting of eleven regiments [approximately eight thousand men], struck their tents and embarked; and the fleet of near one hundred sail fell down to the [Sandy] Hook."[340]

The number of soldiers quartered, fed and drilled on Staten Island's open fields was astounding when compared to its population, which in 1756 was just 2,132.[341] Apparently, good soldiers did not always make good neighbors, and there were numerous reports of pilfering and disorder, including damage done to the Duxbury Glebe, for which the parishioners of St. Andrew's sought and received substantial compensation.[342] There was, however, at least one instance that brought honor and prestige to the county during the war: the first ever investiture of a royal distinction in the Western Hemisphere. On October 25, 1761, a grand ceremony was held in the main British camp during which Sir Jeffery Amherst received the Order of Bath from George III through his proxy, the governor of New York.[343]

SOWING THE SEEDS OF DISCONTENT

As the familiar history goes, in an effort to recover lost revenue and settle the debt from the Seven Years' War, the Parliament of Great Britain passed a series of acts to enforce new forms of taxation on its New World colonies. This, in turn, had the consequence of leading to the organization of committees of correspondence, the Sons of Liberty, the publication of *Common Sense*, the Boston Tea Party, the Continental Congress and, eventually, Paul Revere's famous ride. The rest, as they say, is history.

The province of New York, though far less radical than its New England neighbors, was not exempt from the changing views on colonial self-governance and growing unease of the economic pressure from Parliament. The city's faction of the Sons of Liberty, led by Isaac Sears, John Lamb and Alexander McDougall, though sometimes glossed over in the broader context of the Revolution, was no less defiant than its northern neighbors. The group showed its fervor weeks before the Boston Massacre at the Battle of Golden Hill in January 1770, when the New York Liberty Boys squared off against British troops.[344] The Sons of Liberty also erected a Liberty Pole on a spot still marked in City Hall Park. When word came of Lexington and Concord, Sears and his partisans led a grand parade

An eighteenth-century artist's interpretation of the Liberty Boys defending the Liberty Pole on the New York City Commons. *New York Public Library.*

that day, and in the evening, they managed to seize gunpowder and five hundred muskets from city hall.[345]

On Staten Island, the revolutionary fervor was less public and widespread, and it was more common to find those averse to the looming conflict than in New York City. Two of the county's most famous chroniclers, William T. Davis and Charles Leng, published a series of township and county documents from the period that depict business going on as usual. In one example, officials from the town of Westfield met in April 1768 at the home of Isaac Doughty as the Townshend Acts were just beginning to take their toll on the province's merchants, but instead of discussing that, the men spent their time deciding who would serve as the pound master for cattle and sheep and at what age hogs may no longer take to the town's pastures.[346] This pattern mimics that of Queens County, which also had a certain antipathy to the Revolution. The recorded minutes of its own town meetings make no mention of any discussions of provincial matters after 1770.[347]

The venue for expressing discontent at the Crown appears to have been not at public meetings but rather at the pulpit. By this point, the Anglican Church's power was on the rise beyond the island's ecclesiastical realm and into the political one. There was an overarching tendency of Anglican ministers, especially those in New York with origins in the Venerable Society, to view their loyalty to the episcopacy of the church and the institutional authority of the monarchy as one and the same. Despite the fact that the most famous founding fathers were members of the church, in many towns the terms *Anglican* and *Tory* were synonymous.[348]

Therefore, it was in Richmond's religious non-Anglican congregations that public displeasure with Parliament was aired. Chief among the dissenting preachers was the firebrand Reverend William Jackson, who came to the island in 1769 to form the United Reformed Church in the town of

Richmond. From his lectern, he declared Parliament's actions despotic and "simultaneously denounced the British government and the Anglican clergy as immoral tyrants,"[349] explaining to his congregants that resistance to the Crown's religious and civil authority was "righteous and justified."[350]

Conversely, the growth and political dominance of the Anglican Church in the county, and its resulting support for the British government, served to temper any thoughts of unrest. Loyalist ministers were vocal and unwavering. In one dramatic episode just before the Battle of New York, the Reverend Charles Inglis of Manhattan's Trinity Church boldly recited the royal prayers while George Washington and an angry company of militia watched from the nave.[351] On Staten Island, Reverend Richard Charlton preached similarly to the congregation of St. Andrew's, urging them to defer to "God, the monarchy, and one's social 'betters' as a means of maintaining social order."[352]

Richmond County's Anglicans did obediently look to their social "betters" when it came to electing local officers, and they formed an alliance with the island's Moravians to ensure political domination in the 1760s and '70s.[353] Members of the Moravian Church had begun to emigrate from Europe in the 1730s, and by the outbreak of war, just under one thousand were living in the thirteen colonies. Most settled in western New Jersey and eastern Pennsylvania, where other German speakers were common. Only three congregations were established in New York, one on Staten Island.[354] Moravians had been recognized by Parliament and given legal standing in 1749, making it more tolerable to move to the colonies,[355] and for the most part, they were pacifists who wished colonial resentment would not boil over into war. Their large congregation in Manhattan counted members who fell on both sides of the issue of independence, and this was likely true of their members in New Dorp;[356] however, the Staten Island contingent threw its political weight in with the Anglicans.

Essentially, the island was divided into two factions. On one side, Richmond's Anglicans and leading landowning families like the Dongans, Billopps and Seamans stood firmly against severing ties with Great Britain. On the other, the French, Dutch and small farmers likely shared a more independent spirit of mind. Despite the split, the election results were nearly always one sided, and although French and Dutch surnames are listed on the rolls in subordinate positions, the important and most powerful elected offices in the county were all held by Anglicans.[357]

Another factor that may have contributed to the county's bias toward loyalism was that its Anglican preachers and officeholders were part of a broadly organized social network of similarly minded individuals in New York Province. At the same time, the underlying economic conditions of Richmond were strong enough to suppress disenfranchisement of the poor and middle class, which did factor in the rise of the city's Liberty Boys over the decade leading up to the war. Staten Island was generally prosperous, and the overall contentment of its yeomanry left little room for radicalism.[358]

The county's well-to-do were in regular correspondence with the city's upper crust through commercial ventures and frequent governmental gatherings. For example, William Walton, who served as a member of the colonial assembly and as a county judge,[359] was a successful merchant and was famous for hosting extravagant dinners on Staten Island for New York's elite, such as John Watts and Gouverneur Morris. Walton's nephew and heir would marry into the De Lancey family—as near to royalty in the colonial city as any household.[360] The common thought among all classes just before the Revolution, if there was one, seemed to be that if the system isn't broke, it's best not to fix it.

RESISTANCE AND COUNTER-RESISTANCE

In the summer of 1774, the call went out through the committees of correspondence of the thirteen colonies, which had existed since the Stamp Act of 1765, to assemble delegates for a meeting of the First Continental Congress in Philadelphia. Each New York county was expected to either elect its own delegates or approve those put forward by the city. In every other county, elections were held and delegates chosen, even in Queens, where there was an active Tory circle. Only Richmond chose to set itself apart by ignoring repeated requests and consequently was the only county in New York to not send delegates to the first Congress.[361]

The percentage of the population who supported or opposed this decision remains unclear. Clearly though, political factions formed in Richmond County along the fault line of British sovereignty, as was the case in the province at large and in all of the colonies. Generally speaking, the partisans could be described as either Tories, meaning those favoring British rule, or Whigs, the radicals who pushed for independence. Most historians agree that Richmond had one of the strongest, if not *the* strongest, concentrations of Loyalist sentiment in all of New York,[362] and the elections and political battles of the provincial legislature in 1775 and 1776 certainly corroborate that sentiment.

The New Yorkers who attended the First Continental Congress when it gathered in the fall of 1774 were instructed by the New York Assembly to take a conciliatory tone and to make efforts to support a peaceable reconciliation with Britain.[363] The Tory faction in New York, commonly called the De Lanceyites, may not have agreed with British policy, but neither did they want to see the collective boycott that the Congress sought, which would have the unintended result of punishing the province's own commerce.[364] That year, there were only four Tories elected to the assembly, half of whom were from Richmond. Christopher Billop (the family dropped the second *p* in the eighteenth century) and Benjamin Seaman became members of that body and were instrumental in efforts to vote down radical resolutions that were sent over from the First Continental Congress.[365] Ultimately, along with James De Lancey, they led the assembly in a vote against New York's participation in the subsequent Second Continental Congress.[366]

Nonetheless, a boycott of British goods passed Congress, and it required each province to determine how to best implement it. Since the New York Assembly voted against participating in the Second Continental Congress, the province's leading rebels demanded a fresh round of elections for a new legislative body to essentially function as a Whig alternative to the assembly.[367] Amazingly, the Tories put up almost no opposition to this measure in the spring of 1775, nor did they campaign against the candidates themselves. Instead, they tried to ignore it.[368]

Two elections were scheduled. The first, in April, questioned whether or not each county supported a convention to send delegates to the Second Continental Congress, despite the assembly's official decision. The second, in May, was for electing delegates to the new Whig-led New York Provincial Congress.[369]

In the first election, on April 11, Richmond County's Loyalist bent boiled over, and a heavy majority came out against sending delegates.[370] However, by the second election, on May 1, Richmond's voters did choose to send a relatively moderate delegation to the Provincial Congress, namely Paul Michaeu, John Journey, Aaron Cortelyou, Richard Connor and Richard Lawrence.[371] The slight change in sentiment can perhaps be attributed to lower turnout, Whig propaganda or some combination of the two. But it could also be attributed to news reaching the island of the outbreak of fighting at Lexington and Concord on April 19, 1775. Regardless, when the Provincial Congress gaveled in for the first time at the Exchange

Building on Manhattan's Broad Street on May 23, Richmond County's deputies were in their seats.[372]

According to research by Phillip Papas in *That Ever Loyal Island*, Connor and Cortelyou were leaders of the Moravian community and widely supported by their Anglican neighbors. Billop was a close acquaintance of John Journey, his fellow Anglican, as well as Paul Micheau, who also served as the county clerk. Finally, Richard Lawrence was the owner of one of the island's two shipyards and thus financially vested in the province's commercial interests, especially its overseas trade. All supported the effort to reconcile with Britain. Thanks, in part, to their influence, most of the resolutions that came out of the First Provincial Congress were judicious and tempered, reflecting a conciliatory tone as compared to those of other colonies.[373]

For Staten Island, the most trouble came in June, when the Provincial Congress passed a resolution requiring each county to form a Committee of Safety to enforce the Whig laws of both the Provincial and Continental Congresses. These committees became the source of most anger in Loyalist communities during the early years of the war—and the source of most violent commotions. For many, obedience to such entities, which could act as vigilantes with little evidence and little due process, was the true tyranny to which they found themselves subjugated.[374]

The Richmond committee on safety's first task was to produce a list of all residents who refused to pledge their personal adherence to the Continental Association, which was a document produced by Congress to set the terms of a British boycott. There may have been some resistance, but looming over the heads of any hesitant Staten Islander was the order that any failure to comply would trigger severe economic sanctions. Therefore, Richmond County dutifully but cautiously selected a Committee of Safety of moderate residents, comprising George Barnes, Joseph Christopher, Daniel Corsen, Moses Dupuy, David Latourette, Lambert Merrill, Peter Mersereau, Henry Perine, John Poillon, John Tyson and Christian Jacobson as chairman.[375]

Though the province's Loyalists made little effort to oppose the formation of the First Provincial Congress in May, they would not make the same mistake when elections were called for a second meeting later in the year.[376] In Richmond at least, the Tory efforts succeeded. When a countywide meeting was called to elect deputies, the notion was so unpopular that not enough Staten Islanders even bothered to show up to make a quorum.[377]

The Provincial Congress was incensed, and their response to Richmond's Committee of Safety was quite blunt: "Rest assured, gentlemen, that the

The Christopher House, built in 1720, was moved from Willowbrook Road to Historic Richmond Town and was the meeting place of the Richmond Committee of Safety. *Library of Congress.*

neighboring colonies will not remain inactive spectators if you show a disposition to depart from the Continental Union."[378]

The threat partially worked as another election was advertised and held, and this time, a majority of voters showed up. The electorate's resolve on the matter had not changed, however, and they voted against electing a delegation. Thus, when the Second Provincial Congress gaveled in for the first time on December 6, 1775, there were again no Staten Islanders serving in a Whig legislature.[379]

To account for the county's actions, Richmond's Committee of Safety sent a letter outlining its rationale, explaining:

> *Our former conduct in sending Deputies to represent us in the Provincial Congress, was elevated with the encouraging hopes of having...a reconciliation with Great Britain. But, with anxiety we express it, that the hopes of obtaining so desirable an event, is not almost vanished out of our sight; and, instead of which, we behold with horror, every appearance of*

> *destruction, that a war with Great Britain will bring upon us. Under these apprehensions, and in our particular situation, we hope you will view us, and when candidly considered, we trust you will furnish with sufficient reason, for the present, to forbear with us.*
>
> *We wish and pray that if yet any hopes of reconciliation is* [sic] *left, that measures might be adopted, if possible, to obtain that desirable end, in wishing of which we conclude ourselves.*[380]

This indignation caused a ripple in both the Provincial and Continental Congresses, with the latter swiftly censuring Richmond County. From Philadelphia, Congress ordered that after manifesting "their enmity and opposition to the system and measures adopted for the preservation of liberties in America," the citizens of New York must have no personal or financial dealings with Staten Island.[381] The county was effectively boycotted until its residents pledged their loyalty to the General Association and elected deputies to the Provincial Congress.

Whether it was to reconcile with the Provincial Congress or simply buy some time, both Christian Jacobsen and Richard Lawrence appeared in Manhattan before some of New York's most radical Whig leaders, including Alexander McDougall. On the morning of January 12, 1776, Jacobsen entered the room where the province's Committee of Safety was meeting and, on behalf of Richmond's citizenry, "attempted to state their difficulties and fears," declaring that the majority of his neighbors were "friendly to the measures of Congress."[382] Lawrence, whose maritime business would undoubtedly suffer under a boycott, showed up that afternoon and pressed it further.[383]

Nonetheless, Staten Island's Committee of Safety quickly sent notice to the constituency, and one week later, an election was held. Richmond decided that the moderate Richard Lawrence should return to the Provincial Congress, as well as Adrian Bancker,[384] whose family had a large slave-owning cattle ranch near present-day Snug Harbor. He would remain prominent in Richmond politics throughout his life and serve in the state assembly and as surrogate of the county after the war.[385]

Before the Staten Island representatives were permitted to take their seats, the Provincial and Continental Congresses were each concerned that Richmond's citizenry would not swear to the Continental Association. To ensure they did, the Whig leaders were willing to threaten military force. On February 16, Colonel Nathaniel Heard reported to Congress that he was encamped on Staten Island with seven hundred men, stressing, "There has been sundry complaints made of many of the principal men here, threatening they would kill any of the troops that should come on the island to disarm them."[386] Heard was no stranger to suppressing Loyalists; he and his First Battalion of Middlesex minutemen were deployed to Queens County a month earlier "for duty in arresting Tories and disaffected persons."[387]

The show of force worked. The very next day, Lawrence and Bancker informed the Provincial Congress that they had subscribed to the Continental Association, as well as "above seven-eights of the inhabitants" of the county. They ended their letter with an emphatic plea, explaining that the presence of Heard's troops only served to undermine Whig efforts: "We are of the opinion that it will be for the good of the common cause, to stop the proceedings of the Jersey forces, in order to quiet the minds of the people."[388] On February 19, 1776, the two were allowed to take their seats in the Provincial Congress.[389]

A CIVIL ACTION

When Colonel Heard and his seven hundred Middlesex men ferried across the Kills to Staten Island in the winter of 1776, it was only part of his mission to pressure the Tories into pledging to the Continental Association. Their larger purpose was slightly different but also driven by concerns over the island's Loyalists.

In January, ominously sensing that Staten Island could be used as a friendly landing place for the British in advance of an invasion of the city or that the island could serve as a black market channel to resupply British soldiers elsewhere in the colonies, the New York Committee on Safety called on its counterparts across the Hudson for help patrolling the county. It requested that the New Jersey Provincial Congress, then meeting just twelve miles up the Raritan River from the island in New Brunswick, send a detachment of militia to "guard the livestock on Staten Island, and otherwise secure that place from depredations." Heard's company was dispatched immediately to do just that and to "prevent the enemy from landing on said island."[390] The livestock was quickly secured from the British, but it is worth noting that after New York's Provincial Congress received word that Richmond County had sworn allegiance to the association, it ordered the Jersey troops to retreat. This was in spite of the assurances to Lawrence and Bancker that the incursion was no threat and "intended for no other purpose whatsoever."[391]

However, Heard did not withdraw and instead caused further duress. He arrested four Staten Islanders on charges that they, in addition to hurling insults at the militia, were part of a plot to aid the British army and New Jersey Loyalists.[392] Not trusting the Richmond Committee on Safety to actually carry out the investigations, their loyalty was openly questioned by Congress. Heard's men seized Isaac Decker, Abraham Harris, Minah Burger and Richard Conner and brought them to jail in Elizabethtown to await trial. The Richmond committee protested. The New York Provincial Congress demanded their return. New Jersey reluctantly sent them back,[393] and they faced a trial on the island on March 7, 1776, which was described by contemporaries as a farce.[394] Richmond took care of its own.

This action was just one example that underscores the idea that the Revolutionary War, in many parts of the country and especially in Richmond, more closely resembled a civil war than a war against foreign occupiers. For Staten Island, during the jittery years of 1775 and 1776, just before the British landed and while events unfolded in New England, there were many internecine confrontations placing its Loyalist citizens at odds with their colonial neighbors.

Incidents of violence, suspicion, accusations and condemnations among the populace began early in 1775. By that time, Staten Island's sentiments toward reconciliation with Britain and its general aversion to an armed conflict were well known. Perhaps as important, it was also long recognized by civil authorities as a refuge for smugglers who long used the island's maze of inlets and kills to evade New York's tax collectors. There may have been no better location to offload contraband while a ship lie at anchor than the sparsely populated island at the center of the bay. It was perhaps the combination that its residents were both entrenched partisans and willing to skirt the law that made it somewhat foreseeable that political drama and partisan unrest would envelop Staten Island during the war.

It came as no surprise when smuggling rumors surfaced early that year after two British merchant ships, the *James* and the *Beulah*, were prohibited from offloading their cargo anywhere in New York Harbor. The whispering claimed that illicit merchandise was shuttled ashore by some enterprising Staten Islanders either trying to make a small profit or, more seriously, as part of a British plot.[395] In fact, the *Beulah*'s owners did secretly unload a portion of their cargo in one of the island's inlets so that it could be ferried across the kill to Elizabethtown, New Jersey. The scheme was uncovered, and investigations on both sides of the water produced confessions from the guilty parties.[396]

The accusations and investigations only served to inflame the growing suspicions of Staten Islanders by their Whig neighbors in New Jersey. As a result, the Elizabethtown committee of observation passed a resolution on February 13, 1775, to "break off all trade, commerce, dealings, and intercourse whatsoever with the inhabitants of said Island," which has "manifested an unfriendly disposition towards the liberties of America."[397] A week later, the town of Woodbridge followed suit and appointed inspectors to ensure only goods from Richmond's few Whig merchants be permitted at its landing.[398]

On another occasion, anger against Staten Islanders resulted in open violence. According to the *Rivington's New York Gazetteer*, then a leading Tory publication, an Elizabethtown mob seized "a poor Staten Islander" selling oysters that February "for no other crime than because some other people of that ever loyal Island"[399] had assisted in aiding British ships. The mob beat James Johnson, stole his cargo and dragged him to the town center, where they erected a liberty pole and gallows, as the town judge "was, as usual, completely drunk when the riot commenced."[400] It took the efforts of Elizabethtown's leading citizens, including the eventually sober judge, to prevent his death. In return, Johnson was forced to swear a statement exonerating the townspeople.[401]

LATER THAT SPRING, BRITISH vice admiral Samuel Graves prepared to dispatch the sixty-four-gun *Asia* to New York Bay to assist the Tory New York Assembly in reconciling the colonies and "protecting the properties of well disposed Merchants."[402] By the time the ship departed at the end of April, its mission had changed, as the opening shots at Lexington had rung out.

The *Kingsfisher*, a smaller ship that had wintered in the bay, sent word to Graves that "the Major part of the people here are almost in a State of Rebellion."[403] So when the *Asia* finally sailed through the Narrows on May 26, its mission was to secure the harbor, find provisions and await the troop ships for a potential invasion.[404] It would also serve as a powerful reminder of British sovereignty—menacing to some while reassuring to others.

Despite the animosity, the New York Provincial Congress still allowed certain citizens to sell wares to the British warships as long as they did not go toward replenishing the British army engaged in Boston. This proved to be an error of judgment, and it was soon clear that the British navy was not honoring that commitment. An incensed General Washington ordered the practice to stop. The New York Whigs obligingly passed new measures, but

The HMS *Asia* entered the Narrows into New York Bay on May 26, 1775, as an assertion of continued British supremacy. *Library and Archives Canada.*

Richmond's smugglers weren't willing to pay them any mind. In one case that September, a merchant was forced to flee to the safety of the *Asia* after he was caught clandestinely provisioning British packet ships with Staten Island livestock and produce.[405]

As the months passed and the likelihood of a British invasion of New York grew ever more likely, Washington understood that Tories who could continue to provide assistance around New York Bay would pose a significant challenge to the defense of the city. The New York committee was tasked to organize patrols of the coastal waters and prevent any and all communication with British shipping.[406]

The following spring, the New York committee received notice from Washington that one such patrol apprehended two individuals for interacting with the *Asia*, one of them being Peter Poillon of Richmond County.[407] The general accused him of provisioning the ship, and the New York committee obligingly put him on trial. In his defense, Poillon claimed he had only come alongside the ship after it fired warning shots and ordered him to surrender his provisions. In addition, he produced a number of witnesses the committeemen deemed reputable to attest that he was a "friend to the liberties of his country."[408] This may have been true, as his eldest brother was a member of Richmond's committee who had sworn to the General Association and another brother, James, was killed by the British during the war.[409] However, the committee only let him off on a technicality. As it turns out, Staten Island was located at such a "remote situation" that they believed him when he claimed ignorance to the rules barring interaction with the British.[410]

Washington and New York's Whig leadership were also concerned with Tory activities on land—a fear that grew with the imminence of a British attack. The island's location at the center of the bay, its Watering Place, its view out to Sandy Hook and its commanding heights over the narrow entry into the harbor made it strategically important. Given the reputation of its citizens, leadership knew that Richmond County could potentially be a problem. When Colonel Heard and his New Jersey Militia disembarked on the island in February 1776, they would only be the first detachment of Whig troops sent to occupy and secure it, much to the resentment of its residents.[411]

Yet, when Washington tapped General Charles Lee to prepare the major defenses of New York City, Staten Island, along with its stocks of water, wood, provisions and livestock, was not part of his central focus. Even Washington seemed more concerned with Long Island—both for its advantageous defensive positions at Brooklyn Heights and the need to disarm its leading Loyalists in advance.[412]

Not everyone agreed, however, and some in Washington's circle suggested Staten Island be fortified to protect the southern approaches to the city. Even the Continental Congress proposed that artillery be posted on its heights, making it difficult and costly should British ships try to navigate the sandy banks of the Narrows. Furthermore, it was Lee himself, after he was relieved of the New York command, who would report to Congress that defending the city would be impossible without a significant force controlling the inhabitants of Staten Island, going as far as suggesting that its children be taken as hostages.[413] That Richmond was not supplied with a sizable garrison proved to be a blunder.

Lee did take precautions to ensure that Staten Island's resources did not fall into the hands of the British. However, harassment and the seizure of private property would prove to be the demise of Lee's command in New York and the cause of deepening Tory sympathies around the province—not just in Richmond. In January 1776, acting on orders from Washington, Lee sent Colonel Heard to Queens County to disarm and arrest leading Loyalists. The result was the opposite of what was intended after the troops mistreated many of the inhabitants of Jamaica and Hempstead towns. They were quickly forced to withdraw after meeting some armed resistance, but instead of changing tactics, Lee authorized more incursions into Loyalist towns. Heard, of course, moved on to Staten Island. At the same time, Connecticut Whig companies undertook similar actions against Long Island's Tories, as did Isaac Sears and his radical Liberty Boys from New York City. Essentially, these "Tory Hunting parties," as they were dubbed, caused not only the dismissal of Charles Lee but also assisted in turning prominent Tories into popular

William Alexander, or Lord Stirling (1726–1783), tried to defend Staten Island in 1776 and led a raid on it against the British in 1780. *New York Public Library*.

leaders, having stood up to perceived Whig tyranny on Long Island and similarly on Staten Island.[414]

Lee's replacement was William Alexander, who claimed a Scottish peerage and was contemporarily styled Lord Stirling.[415] His ascension to the command of the New York defenses coincided with the British evacuation of Boston in March 1776. On St. Patrick's Day, General William Howe loaded his troops onto transport ships and sailed with the fleet out into Massachusetts Bay, while Washington sent a message to Stirling, informing him that the ten-month siege had ended. The ships lingered for ten days before disappearing over the horizon, their destination unknown.[416] Washington assumed the worst—that an invasion of New York was days away. He quickly sent further word to Congress, Stirling and Governor Jonathan Trumbull of Connecticut to rush their best units to New York. Two Maryland rifle companies and one from Virginia were stationed on Staten Island, where Stirling marked a series of earthen fortifications that would never be built.[417]

Stirling had long harbored suspicions of Staten Island. Earlier he ominously wrote to the Provincial Congress that "the enemies of American liberty are very busy on Staten Island, and that some dangerous movements are now going on among them." He personally offered to take two divisions to Richmond to disarm its people.[418] But as the British invasion was expected at any moment, the idea was scrapped. Besides, the Provincial Congress and military commanders needed every available man, and Richmond was ordered to supply its share.

The Committee of Safety organized the county into four military districts, each with its own company.[419] On April 12, 1776, Adrian Bancker informed the Provincial Congress that the county's militia officers were First Colonel Abraham Jones, Second Colonel Cornelius Corsen, First Major Jacob Mersereau, Second Major Cornelius Cortelyou, Adjutant Benjamin Parker, First Lieutenant William Lake and Quartermaster Harmanus Garrison.[420] An earlier letter also listed Nicholas Stillwell as quartermaster.[421]

Still distrusting the Staten Island Militia, Stirling requested that "about four hundred Minute-men from New Jersey be stationed on Staten Island, near the Watering Place" to prevent contact with the British ships and to "keep a constant and vigilant lookout towards the sea."[422] As the hours crept by and news of Boston trickled in, Stirling sent a second letter to the president of the New Jersey Congress the next day begging for troops and a third following just two days after that.[423]

Finally, Stirling was ordered by his superior, Major General Israel Putnam, to march with his own brigade of troops to occupy positions on Staten Island. In advance of his arrival, he wrote to New York's Committee on Safety for assistance in pressuring Richmond's committee and its citizens to accept quartering Whig troops. Islanders were urged to prepare barns, vacant farmhouses or any structure that could house the men, ideally with little inconvenience.[424] Within a few weeks, a sizeable force was amassed, and housing the troops became expensive. Richmond County's leadership peppered the Provincial Congress with requests for reimbursement for the firewood they supplied to the troops.[425]

Logistical costs were soon put on the back burner as rebel troops were put into action. On April 7, 1776, two British patrol vessels used the cover of a heavy fog to put in for replenishment at the Watering Place.[426] That part of the island was guarded by some of Stirling's troops at the Narrows, and a company of Virginia riflemen billeted among North Shore farmers. The Virginians were alerted to the incursion, and a farmer named Wandel guided them to a spot where they could make out the sloop *Savage* lying close to shore as several of its men drew water on land. The riflemen opened fire from a covered tree line and began chasing the seamen down the hill toward the beach. *Savage*'s sixteen guns were quick to respond, halting the charge.[427] William Tryon, the last British colonial governor of New York, witnessed the event from the deck of the *Phoenix*, where he sought refuge from Whig mobs in the city. He recalled hearing the initial shots "that by the help of a spyglass we discovered to be the enemy firing upon the Seamen," and soon thereafter, "the *Savage* began a cannonade which was kept up for some hours. Lord Sterling [*sic*], I am told, headed five hundred men on this attack upon eighteen unarmed seamen."[428]

THESE WERE THE FIRST true shots fired in Richmond County during the American Revolution, but beyond that, they were of little strategic significance. The final reports of the skirmish vary, but it likely resulted in two British deaths and the majority of the eighteen sailors taken prisoner.[429] Regardless, the event made it clear to Whig military leaders that the conflict would next be centered on their defense of New York.[430]

TWICE OCCUPIED

As hostilities with British warships continued and the likelihood of invasion grew, so did the tempers of Whig leaders over the behavior of Staten Island's Tories and the eagerness at which they sought to suppress any subversive actions among them.

Stirling's riflemen arrested a number of Loyalists, including Darby Doyle, a ferryman at the Watering Place, who they accused of warning the British landing party of their surprise attack. Alexander McDonald, a Richmond Tory who would go on to serve in the Royal Highland Emigrant Regiment, saw many depravities fall onto his family after he refused to bend to the Whig authorities.[431] His letters record threats to "skin him alive," while his wife, Susannah, and their children were harassed "with more than savage rudeness" by the soldiers quartered on their property.[432] These incidents became more commonplace, and by May, it was also clear that Staten Islanders were not going to be compensated for the lodgings and supplies they provided. Others complained that their gardens, fields and orchards had been overrun and regularly pilfered by roving bands of men. The Whigs were not making any friends in Richmond County, and they knew it.[433]

Whether Washington believed Staten Island would be the landing site or not, he was keenly aware that its livestock would undoubtedly fall into the hands of British quartermasters once the fleet arrived. He asked the Provincial Congress to take measures to see that this wouldn't happen, and in turn, they directed both Richmond's and Elizabethtown's committees to remove the island's herds. After a lack of cooperation from the farmers and perhaps some deliberate stalling, the general was forced to order Captain Ephraim Manning and the Third Connecticut Regiment to finish the job. Yet, as one militia officer remarked, "Our infamous brethren of Staten Island, instead of assisting the troops…they drove them off into hiding places" in the wooded hollows of the island's interior.[434]

The reason Staten Islanders hid their cattle and somewhat passively accepted similar abuses was largely because they believed relief from Whig leadership would soon arrive in the form of a conquering British army and navy. As Richmond's Loyalists stood on the island's heights on June 29, 1776, they were pleased to see their saviors approaching Sandy Hook on their way to New York Bay. The first convoys of the fleet had finally arrived, and by evening the next day, 130 gunships, ships of the line and troop transports were anchored off Gravesend.[435] An observer from New York City described the scene as "a wood of pine trees trimmed….I thought all London was afloat."[436]

At first, Howe considered a direct assault against rebel strongholds on Long Island. But after learning of the political situation in Richmond County from Oliver De Lancey[437] and taking the wise counsel of a staff officer who served under Jeffery Amherst fifteen years earlier, Howe chose to take advantage of Staten Island.[438] Its proximity to New York, Long Island and the interior of New Jersey made it strategically significant, and its freshwater streams, fertile farms, defendable hills and agreeable population all framed it as the perfect long-term staging area. Its occupation during the war would prove to be the longest by British soldiers of any county in the future United States.

At the end of June, the bulk of the British fleet was still on its way. Its commander was the general's brother, Admiral Richard Lord Howe, another one of the four Howe siblings who served with distinction in the British armed forces. In addition to having supreme command of His Majesty's naval forces, Admiral Howe was also deputized as a peace commissioner and charged with negotiating with Washington and Congress. But a week before he arrived on his flagship *Eagle* and a month before the full force of 450 ships and 32,000 soldiers, sailors, marines and militia was amassed in the bay,[439] his brother set his sights on an amphibious landing at the Watering Place.

The British used their command of New York Harbor to their advantage. Staten Island was quickly surrounded. As *Asia*, *Chatham*, *Centurion*, *Phoenix*, *Rose* and *Greyhound*, with their collective 264 guns, all waited for the right

A sketch of Lieutenant Archibald Robertson of the Royal Engineers from atop the Watering Place captured the moment on July 12, 1776, when Admiral Howe's flagship approached the anchored fleet. *New York Public Library.*

combination of tide and wind to enter the Narrows, Vice Admiral Molyneux Shuldham sent his smaller-keeled ships to plug the kills and inlets. The sloop *Swan* was sent to patrol the waters of Raritan Bay, while *Senegal* occupied the Arthur Kill near Amboy "to Cut off the Communication with New Jersey."[440] The schooner *Tryal* cruised the Kill Van Kull near Elizabethtown for the same purpose.[441]

At noon on July 2, the *Greyhound*, with General Howe on its quarterdeck, along with *Rose* and *Phoenix*, crept slowly through the Narrows. Expecting fire from both sides but receiving none, the general signaled to the rest of the transport ships to follow. Facing a strong tide and weak winds as they worked through the strait, the ships were forced to anchor for several hours. This would have put them well within range had the Americans significantly fortified Staten Island's heights. It wasn't until 7:00 p.m. that the troops finally began to disembark in the midst of a "squally" summer rain.[442] It was a textbook operation—the shipboard guns fired at the few rebels visible on shore, and under their cover, the grenadiers and light infantry were all safely landed by 9:00 p.m.[443] The multiple British accounts are consistent in that none of their troops were killed, and some claimed "two or three hundred men of the enemy surrendered themselves prisoners of war to the first division of grenadiers."[444]

Major Charles Stuart provided the most detailed account of the amphibious assault of Staten Island in a letter to his father, the Earl of Bute:

> *We were ordered to land at the Watering-place, which the Grenadiers and Lt. Infantry did without opposition, and remained the whole night under arms.*
>
> *The next morning we were cantoned in the Villages, and the inhabitants received us with the greatest joy, seeing well the difference between anarchy and a regular mild government; it is supposed we shall stay here, making frequent excursions into the plains.*
>
> *Our situation is by no means despicable; we are in the most beautiful Island that nature could form or art improve, we have everything we want, and six or seven deserters come every day either from Long Island or the Jersies who bring intelligence that the rebels are very discontented, but there is no believing these poor deluded wretches.*[445]

The landing was a clear success for the British, but it was not without its hiccups. On July 3, the troops pushed west along the road that ran along the Kill Van Kull to Decker's Ferry (now Port Richmond), marching under the cover of the schooner *George* and a smaller ship that hugged the coast.[446] The rebel riflemen weighed their options, but with "the Inhabitants being unfriendly & the Enemy so near,"[447] Captain Manning decided to withdraw. By 3:00 p.m., in sight of the British ships, the last of his men made it across to New Jersey. From there, along the marshy shoreline opposite the ferry, the Connecticut men dragged a small three-pounder to the water's edge and opened fire. The short barrage was successful, killing one man and wounding four on the decks of the *George*, and required the ship to retire for repairs.[448]

At General Nathanael Greene's camp in Brooklyn, he reported hearing "smart fire at the Westward of Staten Island" in the early morning of July 5 and assumed it was part of additional small engagements. More significantly, his own men were able to capture four prisoners while sneaking around the Narrows overnight, including a captain who was able to provide critical information about the coming attack. As Greene could now confidently confirm to Washington, the men landing on Staten Island were just the beginning, and another twenty thousand men were fast on the way with an additional fleet.[449]

Another captured soldier provided Greene with even more detail of the situation on Staten Island, and the report of his interrogation leaves a thorough record. James MacFarlan, of the Fifty-Fifth Regiment of Foot under General

James Grant, was part of the first battalions that landed on Wednesday, July 3. In total, nine thousand troops landed, including, by his estimate, one thousand who were sick or incapacitated from scurvy or "the Bloody flux" (dysentery).[450] He attested that Richard Lawrence visited the British ships just after they came into Raritan Bay to share intelligence that "there was nobody on the other side of the Island but a small parcel of Jersey rascals."[451]

Grant acted on this tip by immediately marching southwest, and MacFarlan reported that his brigade "is about 1½ Mile from Blazing Star [Rossville] in Land, with three Batalions [*sic*] of 8 Co[ompanies] each,"[452] a total of about 850 men. Separately, he believed "the Grenadiers & light Infantry [were] in a Brigade by themselves in the Middle of the Island." Furthermore, the army's light cavalry units were left behind at Halifax, and the soldiers under Grant had not yet constructed any earthwork defenses. He bluntly told Green, "If they are to be attacked now is the Time,"[453] although no attempt was made.

MacFarlan also discussed the attitude of the soldiers and the civilians of Richmond: "The Inhabitants of Staten Island are well and no Soldier dare do anything [against] them." When a group broke into the home of a known Whig who fled to Jersey (most likely Joshua Mersereau) and commandeered his wine, they were immediately court-martialed.[454] MacFarlan also opined the divided sentiments in the British army on the war, claiming the Scottish and Irish troops, like himself, were "very easy about the Dispute and rather let it alone," while "the English are very violent."[455]

A WELCOME RECEPTION

Staten Island's militia was organized under orders from the New York Provincial Congress just months before for the intended purpose of defending the county from invasion. Yet when the invasion occurred, they did not put up a fight. Instead, on July 6, in a field near Richmondtown, Christopher Billop led Staten Island's four companies in swearing in as members of the British Provincial troops.[456] Joining the militiamen in the elaborate ceremony, which was attended by both Howe and Governor Tryon, were one hundred or so additional Loyalist refugees from New Jersey who were equally eager to serve king and country. Billop was given the rank of lieutenant colonel and placed in command of this ragtag group that was restyled Billop's Corps of Staten Island Militia. Its stated mission was to defend the island and provide auxiliary support for the regular troops. Isaac Decker was appointed its captain in charge its cavalry.[457] This was almost certainly the first group of Tory enlistees from New York, which by the end of the war, would be the greatest source of colonial enlistments of "old Country men" for units like the Royal Highland Emigrants in the Western Hemisphere.[458]

Billop also helped the British gear up for the war effort by organizing a civilian workforce on the island to provide logistics and raw materials to British quartermasters. More than anything else, Howe needed boats. He turned to Richard Lawrence, naming him master carpenter. Lawrence turned his shipyard into a factory for small flatboats for the coming invasion of Long Island. He was also granted the rank of captain and was allowed to patrol the waters around Staten Island for Whig vessels and supplies.[459]

Richmond County's yeomanry, many of whom were not partisans on either side, shared in the war profits from the British encampment. Decker's first assignment was to scour the island for farmers willing to sell their cattle to feed Howe's troops. None were taken by force, and all were compensated. The British cattle herd was driven to the Watering Place, where all of the fences of the Duxbury Glebe were knocked down to create one large grazing area secured with sentries.[460]

For the most part, the soldiers returned the hospitality shown by the island's citizens. Among the firsthand accounts that survive is one from a thirteen-year-old boy who remembered his first encounter with soldiers visiting his hamlet a few days after landing when they demanded something to eat. He recalled, "When they finished they each threw down a half-dollar, to the great surprise of the people."[461] In another incident, Moses Van Name had been asked to supply some cordwood, and after dropping it off, he was given a small stack of gold coins and ordered to proportionally reimburse those who chopped it.[462]

Wood was a principal commodity, and the British would require great sums for fuel during their stay in New York, which by war's end caused one Staten Islander to remark that its once ample woodlands were "all cleared during the Revolution....Hundreds and Hundreds of acres were cut."[463] The quartermasters created a system whereby Richmond residents were permitted to cut the trees from the properties of Whig sympathizers for sale, but with the availability of British hard currency, greed got the best of them, and nearly all of the island was denuded by the mid-1780s.[464]

The seizure of Whig property was also commonplace during the British occupation. After Howe landed, he set up his headquarters and took up residence at the home of Whig provincial congressman Adrian Bancker

Many of the flatboats used by the British during the landings at Gravesend and Kip's Bay were built by Richard Lawrence on Staten Island. *New York Public Library.*

along the road that ran by the North Shore, not far from the army's main camp at the Watering Place, where the troops were housed in sailcloth tents accommodating three hundred men. From the congressman's home, the general attempted to negotiate with the rebels while still planning the invasion of Long Island and New York City. Bancker, one of the few Whig sympathizers who opted not to flee, was eventually detained on a British vessel in the harbor.[465]

Other Whigs suffered torments even worse than Bancker as the roles reversed, and now it was the British who were on the hunt for insurgents. Cornelius Mersereau was forcibly removed from his home and allegedly beaten. Hezekiah and Abraham Reckhow were arrested in early July, and although Hezekiah was released, his brother was condemned to the notorious prison ship *Jersey*. After the war, many Staten Island Whigs recalled the abuses and harassment that befell their families by their own Loyalist neighbors, who were perhaps just returning the favors from months earlier.[466]

On July 10, Howe's army was in complete control of Richmond County and had established rudimentary fortifications at all of its critical points. Lord Hugh Percy commanded the troops occupying Richmondtown. The first brigade guarded the road from Richmondtown north to the Dutch church in modern Port Richmond. The second brigade camped at Blazing Star, in present Rossville, and the third lined the road along the North Shore from the Dutch Church west to the ferry to Elizabethtown. General Grant and the fourth brigade camped along the road to Amboy near New Dorp. The fifth guarded the Narrows, and the sixth camped on Billop's land on the South Shore. The artillery, provisions and quartermaster corps were all stationed at the Watering Place.[467]

War and Peace

As the summer of 1776 wore on, each day brought more and more reinforcements, and soon the troops on Staten Island would be ready for mobilization. As Washington and the Continental forces focused on defending the heights of Long Island, some Americans pondered the feasibility of an offensive action. Brigadier General Hugh Mercer was one such leader, and he amassed a number of men near Elizabethtown to counterpunch. His scouts reconnoitered three separate British sentry posts on Long Neck near the New Blazing Star Ferry. This was the name of the stretch of land between Fresh Kills and the Arthur Kill, now known as Travis. Mercer received intelligence, likely from the Mersereaus who ran a nearby ferry, confirming the enemy had amassed about six hundred men in the area. The British Tenth Regiment, encamped farther north opposite Elizabethtown, sent a detachment to the shoreline to try to harass the rebel boats as they gathered for the crossing. When they ventured a bit too close to the rebel earthworks on the opposite shore, the British took fire from cannon and small arms. Their leader, Lieutenant Blenerhasset, suffered a near-mortal head wound, and another man was struck in the leg.[468] Nonetheless, despite the loss of surprise, Mercer still ordered the rebel attack to proceed on the three positions in the moonlight of July 18.[469]

Over one thousand Continental troops and Pennsylvania riflemen lined the banks of Thompson's Creek, the early name for the New Jersey inlet just south of the modern Goethals Bridge, where they tried to set off in rickety boats for the two-mile paddle down the Kill. But according to Mercer, "Tempestious [*sic*]" weather blew them back ashore, and he feared "the loss of our whole party, in attempting to cross with such boats as we were provided with."[470] A stalemate set in, with Whig troops lining the Jersey coast as their opposite numbers stood guard on Staten Island.

Mercer did come face-to-face with the British later that month. Admiral Howe sent an envoy across the kill to Amboy under a flag of truce to deliver letters to several provincial governors notifying them of his intention to commence peace talks.[471] He assured "that the Door was yet open for Reconciliation."[472] The American general graciously received *Eagle*'s first lieutenant, Samuel Reeve, and the two breakfasted on the morning of July 15, 1776. By Reeve's account, Mercer "behaved civilly, yet rather dryly," and explained away the coarse fare by quipping that "they had Plenty of Necessities, and did not wish for Luxuries."[473] Reeve derisively replied that it was normal for those who did not have any luxuries to want them.

This attempt at brokering a peace was just one of several that the Howe brothers undertook in earnest in the summer of 1776 as they amassed the largest expeditionary force in history—all encamped throughout the fields, hills and woods of Richmond County. The Howes felt very little personal animosity toward the colonies. They tended to side with British Whigs like Edmund Burke, who believed that the Americans had a fair claim and should be treated fraternally. More intimately, both recalled with fondness how the Massachusetts legislature erected a monument in honor of their eldest brother, who had perished in the battle at Ticonderoga during the Seven Years' War.[474] Still, their entreaties were rebuffed. Even Washington personally refused to accept a heartfelt letter sent by Howe, which implored, "As I trust that a dispassionate consideration of the King's benevolent intentions, may be the means of preventing the further Effusion of Blood, and become productive of Peace and lasting Union between Great Britain and America."[475]

Depending on one's views, the collapse of the diplomacy before the invasion of Long Island could be seen as both a positive and negative. Surely, years of bloodshed would follow, but accepting terms in 1776 would have changed the course of history and the establishment of the United States. One other thing was certain: the spirit of the Whig cause was reaching a peak that month as the news of the Declaration of Independence was disseminated throughout the colonies.

On July 9, in the presence of Washington, the document declaring Americans a free and independent people was read to the ragtag companies of Continental troops assembled in Manhattan on the parade grounds at the Commons.[476] A rowdy mob marched to Bowling Green and toppled a statue of George III. His head was placed on a spike at the Blue Bell Tavern, near the American redoubts, while his body was melted down for some four thousand pounds of lead. A celebration ensued.[477]

Unlike elsewhere in New York, there were no recorded celebratory musket shots or bonfires in Richmond when news of the declaration reached its shores, and the island was almost certainly the location where British commanders first learned of it. As legend has it in *Morris's Memorial History*, General Howe was discussing Staten Island's fortifications with his staff officers at a table at the Rose and Crown (sometimes described as a tavern and other times a farmhouse), which was located near the present intersection of New Dorp Lane and Richmond Road. An excited staff officer rushed over with a copy of a newspaper, and after Howe read the first few lines, he ordered the soldier to read it aloud. As it was read, the general stared outside looking at the rows of tents that rolled off into the beach, and when finished, he stoically remarked, "Those are certainly determined men."[478]

A few days later, after a long night of planning on board the *Eagle* in Raritan Bay, the Howe brothers issued their own proclamation in response. In it, they sought peace and offered leniency. They guaranteed the King's "free and general Pardons to all those, who in the Tumult and Disorder of the Times may have deviated from their just Allegiance, and who are willing, by a speedy Return to their Duty, to reap the Benefits of the Royal Favor."[479]

Their message had little impact on Whig leaders, but more Loyalist refugees continued to trickle onto Staten Island. As visions of peace faded in the distance, a steady stream of British ships arrived in the harbor.

On August 1, General Henry Clinton sailed through the Narrows with several warships, along with Lord Cornwallis and eight veteran regiments. When he dropped anchor in the bay, the city he saw through his spyglass was somewhat familiar, as Clinton had spent part of his boyhood in New York when his father served as provincial governor three decades earlier. Days later, a twenty-two-ship convoy from England and Scotland brought several more infantry regiments, and on August 12, a

The Rose and Crown Tavern stood in New Dorp along modern Richmond Road. It was frequently visited by General Howe and was allegedly where he first read the Declaration of Independence. *New York Public Library.*

fleet of more than one hundred ships sailed into New York Bay. Their holds housed nearly nine thousand Hessian mercenaries. General Howe now had a grand total of twenty-four thousand troops in twenty-seven regiments, all supported by over ten thousand seamen who could bring 1,200 guns of the Royal Navy to bear on Washington's scrappy troops defending the city and Long Island.[480]

For the men, however, all was not smooth sailing. When the Hessians landed, they were forced to set up a separate camp on Staten Island. This was not simply a result of, according to one British officer, their "being Foreigners" and "naturally dirty," but rather because "they had not been a Week on Shore before there was between 7 & 800 Men very ill, with Fevers, Diarrhea, & Scurvy."[481]

Nonetheless, Howe began loading up the troops onto transports and barges on August 18, but because of bad weather, it took several days to get the initial fifteen thousand men afloat. At 9:00 a.m. on August 22, Admiral Howe fired a signal gun from *Eagle*'s quarterdeck, and the first wave of four thousand veterans under Clinton and Cornwallis rowed to the Gravesend shore. *Phoenix*, *Rose* and *Greyhound* aligned their broadsides to the shore, while the aptly named bomb ships *Carcass* and *Thunder* prepared their mortars. Wave after wave of men, machines and animals followed.[482]

By Admiral Howe's own account, all fifteen thousand men were landed before noon, and of the "Diligence and Utility" of his officers commanding the landing, "too much Commendation could not be bestowed."[483] Meanwhile, General Howe was quickly gaining ground and requested "that some Diversion might be attempted by the Ships" under his brother's command, and soon, he outflanked the Americans in what's known as the Battle of Long Island.[484]

On August 25, 4,300 Hessians, along with their artillery and wagon trains, crossed the Narrows and joined the main force. This left between 3,000 and 4,000 soldiers to garrison the island and provide a potential diversionary attack into New Jersey.[485] More importantly, with Richmond County still serving as the British headquarters near the front lines, it would be the scene of one of the most consequential diplomatic events of the war.

Diplomacy's Collapse

The Battle of Long Island was a disaster for Washington. On August 29, he convened a council of war at his Brooklyn Heights headquarters as Howe's land forces pushed the Continental troops back against the waters of the East River while the British navy closed off the approaches. The view of his assembled officers was unanimous. To save the army, it must immediately retreat to Manhattan.[486]

In what could be considered the only successful American maneuver of the battle, the troops began a covert retreat that night at 8:00 p.m. One thousand men kept the American campfires burning and were prepared to make a gallant stand should the enemy cavalry overcome the retreat. Down at the shoreline, newly minted General Alexander McDougall stood on a ferry dock, near the site now used as the Brooklyn Bridge Ferry dock, where he orchestrated the embarkations in silence and without lanterns. By daybreak, the army had been miraculously saved, and the Continental troops could see their astounded British counterparts occupying the redoubts where they stood just hours before.[487]

Days went by as Howe's men lined the banks of the East River and the navy positioned itself to cover a potential crossing, but none came. Once again, with the might of the British forces poised to attack, Admiral Howe attempted a peaceful resolution.

He turned to a captured enemy general, John Sullivan, to serve as his emissary. On August 30, just after the British realized the Americans had escaped, the burly Irish American was allowed to enter New York under a flag of truce to confer with Washington.[488] That afternoon, he reported to Howe that Washington had no power to engage in peace talks "but has not the least objection to my going to Philadelphia to Inform Congress."[489] Howe urged his immediate departure.[490]

Congress weighed the matter for a few days before electing to send a delegation, although the resolve to seek peace was not universally shared. John Adams was incensed at the notion that the general was a willing participant in the effort and reportedly muttered under his breath that he "wished the first shot fired by the British in the Battle of Brooklyn

On September 11, 1776, Admiral Howe failed to negotiate a peace with Benjamin Franklin, John Adams and Edward Rutledge at a meeting at the Billop or Conference House. *New York Public Library.*

had gone through Sullivan's head."[491] To his wife and closest confidant he reported, "It would fill this Letter Book, to give you all the Arguments, for and against this Measure,"[492] and although he was personally opposed to the peace conference, his view was in the minority. In the end, Congress decided not only to send a delegation but also that Adams, himself, should be part of it, along with Benjamin Franklin and Edward Rutledge.

The party set out even before the site of the meeting was established. But with the British encamped on Staten Island and its position near the main routes between Philadelphia and New York, it was an obvious choice. Franklin suggested two spots to the admiral: "either at the House on Staten Island, opposite to Amboy, or at the Governor's House in Amboy, we might be accommodated with a Room for the purpose." He promised to be at Amboy on the morning of September 11.[493] Still unsure of the location, he also wrote to his grandson from the road, urging him to forward any messages to him by horseback, "thus if N[ew] York should be the Place, we may not go so far out of our way as Amboy would be."[494]

On September 10, the party sought lodging in Brunswick, but nearly all of the inns were full. Adams and Franklin were forced to share a single bed in a tiny room with one small window, which became the subject of an argument over whether it should remain open or shut. Adams recorded in his diary that Franklin rambled on about the virtues of fresh air for so long that the conversation put both men asleep.[495]

At 9:00 a.m. on Wednesday, September 11, 1776, the party of Adams, Franklin and Rutledge stood on the Amboy shoreline and was greeted by the admiral's barge. Lord Howe was waiting for them at the Manor of Bentley, then owned by Christopher Billop and built by his great-grandfather nearly one hundred years earlier. Howe had sent one of his officers as a hostage to guarantee their security, but the Americans agreed that it would be "childish" to rely on such a pledge and took the man on board the boat with them. As they approached the Staten Island beach, Lord Howe walked down the sloping grassy field to the shoreline, where he formally received the delegation.[496]

Adams described the scene in vivid detail:

> *We walked up to the House between Lines of Guards of Grenadiers, looking as fierce as ten furies, and making all the Grimaces and Gestures and motions of their Musquets with Bayonets fixed, which I suppose military Ettiquette requires but which We neither understood nor regarded.*
>
> *The House had been the Habitation of military Guards, and was as dirty as a stable: but his Lordship had prepared a large handsome Room, by spreading a Carpet of Moss and green Spriggs from Bushes and Shrubbs in the Neighbourhood, till he had made it not only wholesome but romantically elegant, and he entertained Us with good Claret, good Bread, cold Ham, Tongues and Mutton.*[497]

Howe seemed to get along better with Franklin than Adams. He called Adams a "decided Character" after the future president smugly told the admiral to formally address him in any fashion, "except that of a British Subject."[498]

His interactions with Franklin, although more intimate and pleasant, also did not result in any meeting of the minds. Lord Howe expressed profuse gratitude for the people of Massachusetts for the tribute to his deceased brother and opined, "If America should fall, he should feel and lament it, like the Loss of a Brother."

Franklin kindheartedly replied, "My Lord, We will do our Utmost Endeavors, to save your Lordship that mortification."

Howe appreciated the mutual respect and perhaps he wanted to believe it. Yet his only response was, "I suppose you will endeavor to give Us employment in Europe," a clear reference to Congress's attempt to get France involved in the war. To that, the delegation gave "not a Word nor a look."[499]

Officially, the Staten Island peace conference of 1776 failed. Lord Howe made it clear that he did not have, nor likely would he ever have, the power to acknowledge the colonies as independent states. His mission was to restore order and issue pardons. The American delegation would not and in fact lacked the authority to consent to any agreement that did not accept the separation of the two continents as a precondition. Although the conversation would go on for three hours and cover several sensitive topics including the economic costs, the powers of the Crown and the rights of the governed, it ended as politely as it began. The admiral summed "that if the Colonies would not give up the System of Independency, it was impossible for him to enter into any Negociation." They parted ways.[500]

Four days later, the guns of *Phoenix*, *Rose*, *Roebuck*, *Orpheus* and *Carisford* opened with a barrage at a small detachment of Connecticut troops guarding Kip's Bay on Manhattan Island. For an hour, they rained cannon and grape shot "so terrible and so incessant a Roar of Guns few even in the Army & Navy had ever heard before."[501] Forty-five hundred troops hidden on flatboats in the Newtown Creek spilled out into the East River and by noon had rowed through the smoke toward their landing. The Americans who did not flee were left either wounded or dead in the shattered remains of their earthworks. When the British set foot on Manhattan Island, no one could have foreseen that it would be seven long years of bloodshed before the war's end.

5

THE BRITISH ISLE

In August 1776, the crux of the war left the shores of Staten Island. Although there would not be major engagements on the scale of Yorktown or Brandywine, British soldiers would remain, with good reason, firmly planted in Richmond County until 1783. For British command, the island was both tactically and strategically significant. It would serve as a launch point for offensive incursions into New Jersey, and defensively, it acted as a buffer against American commanders attempting harassing actions against New York City. Plus, fortifying the Watering Place and the Narrows would ensure the protection of British shipping. This meant that for almost the entirety of the war, the Arthur Kill and the Kill Van Kull would be the line between Continental and British troops.

For the Howe brothers, Richmond's Loyalist citizens were another asset. Its Tories were eager and willing to assist the logistical work of British quartermasters in New York City, especially if it meant payment in British currency. The relative safety also gave military leaders a place where they could convalesce war-worn troops, and its fields could stage and train units for new operations. In 1776, Howe would leave only two brigades to garrison the island: one brigade of the Fourteenth Regiment of Foot and another newly formed brigade of formerly convalescent troops. To supplement these regulars, he relied on the Staten Island Militia and its cavalry and designated the county as the headquarters of the New Jersey Volunteers and the Queen's Rangers, two of the largest and most important Loyalist regiments recruited during the war. Additionally, a number of different units of British regular troops and Hessian mercenaries would rotate on and off Staten Island.[502] In short, Richmond County was critical to the British war effort.

Howe and his successors also used Staten Island to treat the sick and wounded. The most severe cases were most certainly camped at a place then called the Orchard, which was previously part of Dongan's Castleton estate and is now the approximate site of the West Brighton Houses.[503] Several skeletons attributed to British and Hessian soldiers were exhumed early in the nineteenth century during construction in the area, indicating that it served as the burial ground of the terminally ill.[504]

In the 1850s, Staten Island professor Charles Anthon interviewed a series of octogenarians who each gave an account of their war memories. Many recalled that convalescing soldiers, either from illness or exhaustion, were a large part of the island's garrison. Often, they would compose whole units arriving from Europe who, after a lengthy sea journey, were ordered by the general to be "disembarked upon Staten Island to refresh for a short Time."[505] The practice proved worthwhile and continued for several years. As Admiral Howe put it, "It was…found expedient to land them first for their Refreshment on Staten Island; When they became entitled to the full Proportion of Victualing, similar to the Rest of the Army."[506]

A few days on the solid earth of Richmond County was a welcome change for most soldiers who had been cooped up in rocky transport ships for several weeks during an Atlantic crossing. Of course, not everyone shared in the joy on Staten Island. Private Johann Conrad Döhla of the Fourth Company of the Hessian Beyrouth Regiment recorded, "The climate here on Staten Island and in the northern regions of America in general is rather different from ours.…In the day, the great heat causes suffocation and death. On the other hand, at night it is as cold as if it were fall. Above all, the air, because of the frequent fog from the nearby ocean and the foul fumes on Staten Island, is highly unhealthy. Therefore, sickness such as putrid fever, diarrhea, and dysentery often spread through our regiment, and half the men were ill."[507]

PARTISANS

Even if the environment wasn't preferred by some Europeans, the political climate of the island and its position on the front lines between the main bodies of British and American forces made it an attractive option for partisan bands throughout the region.

Combat in Richmond County, like that in Westchester and Bergen Counties, was fought with similar tactics to what was common in the southern backcountry, where partisan bands engaged in an almost endless civil war. Staten Island's resources were exploited, and its residents were caught in the middle of a struggle that they had once hoped to avoid. Whig bands would repeatedly cross the kills on quick raiding missions, while Tory sympathizers and refugees traversed those same lines for protection among the growing corps of Loyalist units billeted on the island or even to join up themselves.[508]

For many blacks, arriving in Richmond County could be the first step toward a permanent freedom. With the promise of manumission from British provincial governors, hundreds flocked to the island during the course of the war. This caused unplanned tensions, as the county's Loyalists were often also slave owners themselves. To keep from losing their support, Howe and his successors offered freedom in exchange for service to only those slaves fleeing Whig masters. The British took particular pains to enforce this and rounded up fugitive slaves and returned them to their allied masters.[509]

Initially, the black refugees were housed in segregated camps and limited to performing labor-intensive logistical work for the British army. But as the need for fighting men grew, they were soon welcome to train and join new black units commanded by white officers. Two regiments were formed and periodically billeted on Staten Island: the Black Pioneers and the Black Brigade. Both were mobilized for action in conjunction with other provincial units.[510]

Overall, the largest provincial unit raised and trained on Staten Island was the New Jersey Volunteers, recruited predominately from British sympathizers who had fled Whig control of their home communities. It was also called Skinner's Brigade after its commander Cortlandt Skinner, a prominent New Jersey politician who quickly rose from colonel to brigadier general, or Skinner's Greens, for their large green wool overcoats. Two thousand men joined, forming six battalions,[511] and they would remain on Staten Island for most of the war. Outside of a deployment to the South, there is little evidence that they ever strayed too far beyond Staten Island's shores. Skinner located his headquarters in the Kreuzer-Pelton House, which is still standing in Randall Manor along Richmond Terrace. During the war, he entertained the famous Major John Andre, and rumor has it that the young sailor-prince who would later become King William IV frequented the home.[512]

The other large provincial unit based in Richmond County was the Queen's American Rangers, which was originally formed during the French and Indian War. In the years separating the two conflicts, Major Robert

Rogers, its legendary original commander, faced court-martial, banishment, debtor's prison and financial ruin. In an effort to restore his fortune and fame, he initially sought a commission with the Americans. Not only did they reject him, but they also imprisoned him, although he quickly managed to escape from a Philadelphia prison and made it back across British lines. In July 1776, he rowed alongside the *Eagle*, where, to his own surprise, he was greeted warmly by Howe and given permission to again recruit a company of the Queen's Rangers.[513] Just a month later, the papers of a dead Tory spy in Westchester County confirmed that Rogers was already operating under direction from British command.[514]

Initially, the volunteers who joined the Rangers were a mix of farmers, scoundrels and agitators, all looking for adventure and the opportunity to be one of the once-famous Rogers's Rangers. The unit was initially deployed along the North Shore of Long Island, harassing coastal towns and crossing the sound for raids on Connecticut. Most famously, it was Rogers who captured the young Nathan Hale in disguise near his headquarters at Flushing.[515] The Rangers spent the winter of 1776–77 participating in the fighting around Westchester, when Roberts was removed from his command in a reshuffling of provincial officers.[516]

By late 1777, the Queen's Rangers were placed under the command of Lieutenant Colonel John Graves Simcoe as they were taking part in Howe's campaign to seize Philadelphia. Months later, after participating in the Battle of Monmouth and other engagements near New York City, the Rangers landed on Staten Island in October 1778. Simcoe ordered his men to destroy the huts used to house the "sickly" regiment they relieved and set up a camp from which they would operate for two years, until December 11, 1780.[517] He made his headquarters the stately home of the LaTourette family,[518] which stood near the crest of Richmond Hill, about a quarter mile northwest of Richmond Town, where the outline of the access road can still be seen cutting into the hillside. The former home site is just behind the present-day golf course driving range, where there is still evidence of its foundation and wells. (The existing brick house of the golf course was built by David LaTourette around 1830.)[519]

Simcoe's reputation had reached the shores of Staten Island long before his regiment arrived. By 1778, Tories had already heard of his gallantry, and rebels were well aware of his savagery. His fame grew out of the regiment's actions around Philadelphia and Germantown and for being the last troops to escape from Sandy Hook after the Battle of Monmouth. When he set out to replenish the ranks of the Queen's Rangers on Staten Island, he ordered

John Greaves Simcoe commanded the Queen's Rangers in Richmond County during the American Revolution and was responsible for the construction of the British fortifications above Richmond Town. *New York Public Library.*

monthly advertisements in the *Royal Gazette* to print the name of its famous commander, "Lieutenant Colonel Commandant J. GREAVES SIMCOE," in the largest font, even outsizing the name of the King.[520]

While men came to the island from all over to serve in the Queen's Rangers, the bulk of Richmond County's homegrown Tory partisans served under Christopher Billop. As previously mentioned, four hundred men joined the initial band of county militia and, on Howe's landing, "cheerfully…took the Oath of Allegiance & fidelity to his Majesty."[521] A few days later, Governor Tryon ordered another muster of fresh provincial recruits "for the defense of the Island as the General finds it an important Quarter to hold against the Rebels."[522]

In addition to Isaac Decker's appointment as captain of cavalry in Billop's Corps, there are many more names of its officers who would be familiar to modern Staten Islanders: Bedell, Seaman, Manee, Coleman, Conner and a young trumpeter named Alfred Poillon.[523]

Volunteers did trickle in from elsewhere in the region, but Billop's cavalry and infantry corps always managed to contain a majority of native islanders.

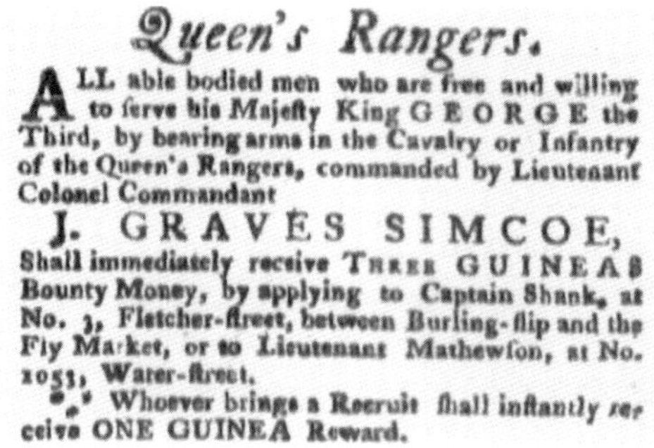

Queen's Rangers.

ALL able bodied men who are free and willing to ſerve his Majeſty King GEORGE the Third, by bearing arms in the Cavalry or Infantry of the Queen's Rangers, commanded by Lieutenant Colonel Commandant

J. GRAVES SIMCOE,

Shall immediately receive THREE GUINEAS Bounty Money, by applying to Captain Shank, at No. 3, Fletcher-ſtreet, between Burling-ſlip and the Fly Market, or to Lieutenant Mathewſon, at No. 1053, Water-ſtreet.

, Whoever brings a Recruit ſhall inſtantly receive ONE GUINEA Reward.

While garrisoned in Richmond County, the Queen's Rangers actively recruited, placing newspaper ads highlighting Simcoe's name in New York's *Royal Gazette*. *New York State Library.*

Among the list of infantry privates, the muster roll lists many more prominent Staten Island family names—some repeated several times as brothers and cousins joined together. There were nine Simonsons, six Manees, four Bedells, four Conners, four Housmans, four LaTourettes, four Laforges, three Egberts, three Tottens, two Poillons, two Spraggs, two Corsens, two Deckers, two Perines, two Stillwells and two Van Names. Additionally, there was a Bodine, DuBois, Cubberly, Journeay, Merrell, Garrison, Androvette, Barton, De Hart, Prall and Van Pelt.[524]

Colonel Billop also outfitted a small gunboat for patrolling the kills to cut off communication and smuggling. Bayles's *History of Richmond County* records a receipt for eighty-one pounds for the vessel and a crew of eight as of September 1779.[525] It was a small sailboat outfitted with two gun mounts on deck and was light enough to work its way well into Richmond Creek.[526] The boat was notorious for its harassment, and "[i]t was an almost daily occurrence that those on board fired at any person within their reach on the Jersey shores."[527] It was commanded by Captain James Stewart and Lieutenant Bornt Randall, and its crew contained yet more members of the Bedell, Simonson, LaTourette and Laforge families.[528]

FORTRESS BRITANNIA

For the most part, British and Hessian soldiers were happy to be on Staten Island and among its approximately 3,500 friendly residents. With the exception of the previously quoted Private Döhla, most mentions in letters are of the county's beauty, its topography and the warmth of its Tory majority. In a letter to a politician back home in Hesse-Kassel, Lieutenant Johann von Hinrich gave this description in September 1776:

> *Staten Island is a hilly country, covered with beautiful forests composed mostly of a kind of fir tree, the odor of which can be inhaled at a distance of two miles from land. The island, itself, however, is but sparsely settled. The soil is fruitful. Peaches, chestnuts, apples, pears, grapes, and various kinds of nuts grow here in wild profusion, mingled with roses and blackberry bushes. The climate and soil are, without exception, the loveliest, healthiest, and most agreeable on the face of the globe: and a person, were he so disposed, could easily lay here the foundations of a great fortune for his progeny should he invest a reasonable sum in land. Just about this time everything is still in an uncivilized and poverty-stricken state, for the foraging parties of the rebels and the different encampments of his Majesty's troops have stripped the country of all the necessary articles of life. The so called "Old and New-Town" consists of two houses scarcely 25 feet square, the walls and roofs of which are covered with boards. The soldiers have eaten up most of the horned cattle hereabouts, but what few are left are very good eating. The houses are miserable. The inhabitants are mostly descendants of Hollanders, and for this reason the German language is pretty well known here.*[529]

As Howe's regiments settled into the island's comforts, it soon became clear that it must be fortified from incursions and sporadic raids from New Jersey. These kinds of short attacks were fairly common, and Döhla's diary also describes one such incident in 1777. He was camped in tents near the Watering Place when they encountered an enemy raiding party. He wrote, "8 June. During the night, at about nine o'clock, our picket was alarmed for the first time, and some shots were exchanged without causing any damage. A few rebels in boats crossed the Kills River and fired several times at our outposts, returned to their boats, and left, and this they often do so that there is no rest in camp at night."[530]

The British garrison required protection against these limited incursions, and command decided to construct a series of earthen redoubts, lookout posts and artillery batteries. Soon after their first landings on Staten Island in 1776, work began. But most astonishingly, the first thing British soldiers noticed after their initial landing was that the rebel troops failed to arm whatever primitive earthworks they managed to erect near the Narrows and Watering Place. "The enemy had no cannon upon these posts," Major Charles Stuart remarked. "Had they, we must have been annoyed most prodigiously."[531]

British officers quickly ordered a survey of the heights above the Watering Place so that it could be further strengthened. A sketch made on July 15,

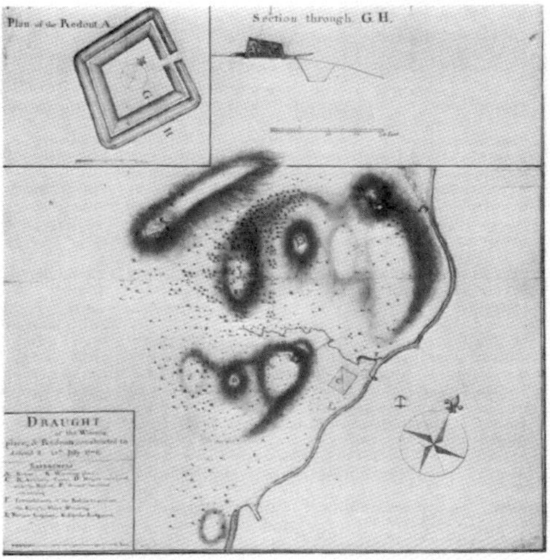

Watering Place and Redoubts on Staten Island.

Unlike the rebels, the British fortified the Watering Place almost as soon as they landed, according to this sketch made on July 15, 1776. *From* Naval Documents of the American Revolution, *vol. V.*

1776,[532] as well as nineteenth-century archaeological and testimonial evidence, help mark the location of three separate redoubts. Envisioning the land cleared of trees and without their modern buildings, each would have provided commanding views and mutually supportive positions over the shoreline.

Two redoubts were situated on Fort Hill, and the larger sat on what was once called Knyphausen Heights, named for the Hessian general stationed there for many months. It was square with eighty-foot sides and stood fifteen feet tall from the bottom of its ditch.[533] The exact location was at the top of Fort Place, including the property now part of Fort Hill Park.[534]

The second redoubt on Fort Hill was slightly smaller and on a gentler rise approximately three hundred yards southwest of its neighbor. This fortification was still visible in the late nineteenth century and was marked on an 1874 atlas at the crest of Scribner, Winter and Bismark Avenues, near the small city park.[535] This earthwork was circular with a diameter of about seventy-five feet.[536]

The third fortification at the Watering Place was a semicircle entrenchment atop Pavillion Hill. The plot had a wide view of the bay and could serve as both a lookout point and artillery platform.[537] It was steep then, as it is today, and even modern streets do not directly ascend its front slope above Saint Paul's Avenue. The houses along the eastern ridge of Thompson Circle still have the same vantage point above Tompkinsville.[538] The British and Hessian soldiers of its garrison built their lodgings by digging into the side of the hill near the intersections of Van Duzer Street and St. Paul's Avenue. These dwellings, essentially dug-out caves shored up with planks, were also visible to Staten Islanders until the 1830s.[539]

In 1777, Sir Henry Clinton was passed over in favor of "Gentleman Johnny" Burgoyne for command of the northern army heading to Albany. After the defeat at Saratoga, he may have been relieved that he was not in charge, but early that summer, Clinton was unhappy to have been left behind to defend New York City while the new campaign in the North began and Howe took the bulk of his main force to seize Philadelphia.[540] With a skeleton garrison, Clinton endeavored to make improvements to the harbor's defenses. He dispatched the army's chief engineer, John Montresor, to survey and improve existing fortifications, including specific plans for Staten Island.

Under Montresor's direction, the fortifications around the Watering Place were strengthened. On July 3, 1777, his journal records his order for a work party of 150 men to construct fascines for the rear of each redoubt. He also ordered two small redoubts built "for 30 men each to terminate the flanks" and placed "6 Iron 6 pounders" on the heights, each with three hundred rounds.[541]

The following summer, Montresor led Clinton on a tour of the high points of the Narrows "on Staaten and Long Island and gave my Project for defending that Pass."[542] *Morris's Memorial History* marks the spot as being that of modern Fort Wadsworth,[543] and there is also a firsthand account of who occupied it. Simcoe notes in 1779 that "Colonel Lord Rawdon, with the volunteers of Ireland, was quartered near a redoubt at the point of the narrows."[544]

Morris's history also provides the most extensive list of all British fortifications, and there is some evidence to verify his claims. He asserts that two redoubts were quickly built near Holland's Hook by General Samuel Cleaveland.[545] His presence on the island in 1776 is confirmed in letters, and he is listed as commanding "the Artillery and Broken Corps" on the North Shore.[546] Given the constant threat from New Jersey rebels, it would be impossible to imagine that this spot opposite Elizabethtown would not have been immediately strengthened.

In fact, the entire west coast of the island was likely fortified quickly after the British landed, as harassing fire and raids began as soon as they settled. Four of the six full brigades on the island in July 1776 were positioned to guard different spots along the kills, where the rebels matched their efforts on the Jersey shoreline from Newark to Amboy.[547] There would be at least one thousand men stationed at Rossville that summer, just one of the many posts. To reiterate, the Arthur Kill and the Kill Van Kull were, tactically speaking, the front lines of the American Revolution for over six years. The first skirmishing into this no-man's land began on July 25, 1776, when Colonel Heard, in command of provincials at Amboy,[548] ordered his men to fire on an armed ship. The British response proved more accurate, and the Americans onshore suffered one loss.[549]

There were additional redoubts guarding the coastline and tidal inlets. One was built beneath present-day Richmond Avenue, where it crosses Fresh Kills in Greenridge. At the time, the area was known as the Bedell Homestead, and the British used one of the family's mills as a storehouse.[550] Another earthwork guarded the Blazing Star Ferry from the heights above Rossville, approximately where 2274 Arthur Kill Road is now. Two more completed the line of defenses along the west shore: one near the bend in Kreischer Street, perhaps at the top of the hill by the mansion, and the other by the Billop property opposite Amboy. Along the Raritan Bay shoreline, the British fortified Prince's Bay, where it was common for ships to unload and lay at anchor.[551] The main battery was atop the "Red Bank lighthouse" and was "capable of accommodating several guns."[552] This is a reference to the high red clay cliffs that house the recently landmarked lighthouse in the Mount Loretto Unique Area. On the east side of Prince's Bay, a small redoubt was built on the point of land near the Manee House, which occasionally served as the headquarters of General John Vaughan and other commanders in that area.[553] At one point in July 1777, Prince's Bay served as an embarkation camp for six British regiments and a Hessian brigade as they repeatedly launched incursions into New Jersey.[554] Completing the South Shore defenses, a mile-long stretch of small earthworks was erected along the beaches of New Dorp, where soldiers camped in tents around present-day Miller Field.[555]

Smaller works were also thrown up on the North Shore along the Kill Van Kull, where an estimated twenty guns guarded the small inlets between Snug Harbor and Port Richmond.[556] There was a fifty-foot breastwork near the bend in Richmond Terrace at Pelton Avenue with a redoubt just behind it on Elizabeth Avenue.[557] Another redoubt stood on the spot of the modern Church of the Ascension, and a small fort on the property of Isaac Decker just east of Port Richmond Avenue served as the headquarters of his cavalry unit.[558]

Still, the most significant fortification on the island was at the Lookout Place or Old Fort, names that held on through the nineteenth century. It sat atop Richmond Hill, and since the area was stripped of trees, it had nearly

360-degree views to Raritan Bay, the Arthur Kill and the Richmond Creek. Though it is perhaps hard to visualize now since silt has clogged up the creek and Fresh Kills, in the 1770s, it was a navigable waterway up to St. Andrew's Church and thus an important route of commerce.[559] Believing it was an avenue to attack the county seat, the British fortified their strongest position above the creek and town.

As noted, when Simcoe arrived in 1778, he set up his headquarters at the old LaTourette estate house, just northwest of St. Andrew's Church. The home was just a few hundred yards from the Old Fort, which, in his opinion, had "three bad redoubts, so constructed, at various times and in such a manner, as to be of little mutual assistance: the spaces between these redoubts had been occupied by the huts of the troops, wretchedly made of mud."[560] Simcoe ordered his men to destroy the existing housing and construct log huts that could be used to provide cover if there was any attempt to flank the redoubts. In December 1778, construction was complete, and troops settled in. Just weeks later, it would face its first test.[561]

The location of this fortification is marked on the 1917 Atlas of New York City as the "Old Fort"[562] and as the "Old Fort or Lookout Place"[563] in the 1874 Atlas of Richmond County. At least one of the redoubts was still clearly visible and identifiable at the turn of the twentieth century because historian William T. Davis described it as "overgrown with semi-wild vegetation."[564] Specifically, he said:

> *In outline the old fort is square with the exception that the southwest side facing the Kill bulges slightly.…The corners point north, east, south, and west, and the entrance is on the northeast side which is the most easy of access. On this side also, the hill has been dug away to furnish earth for the embankments, though nearly all signs of the work have now been obliterated. Each side of this rectangular fort measures about forty four feet along the top and on the southwest the descent to the Kill is as precipitous as the nature of the soft crumbling serpentine rock will permit; but from the other points the fort is more approachable.*[565]

This turn-of-the-century description, along with Simcoe's contemporary journal, seems to confirm a diagram sketched on October 30, 1779, now housed at the Library of Congress.[566] The plan notes the dimensions and orientation of three square earthworks—the one Davis described was merely the northeasternmost. Using historical atlases, archaeological records and mapping software, it is possible to determine the precise site. A golfer standing

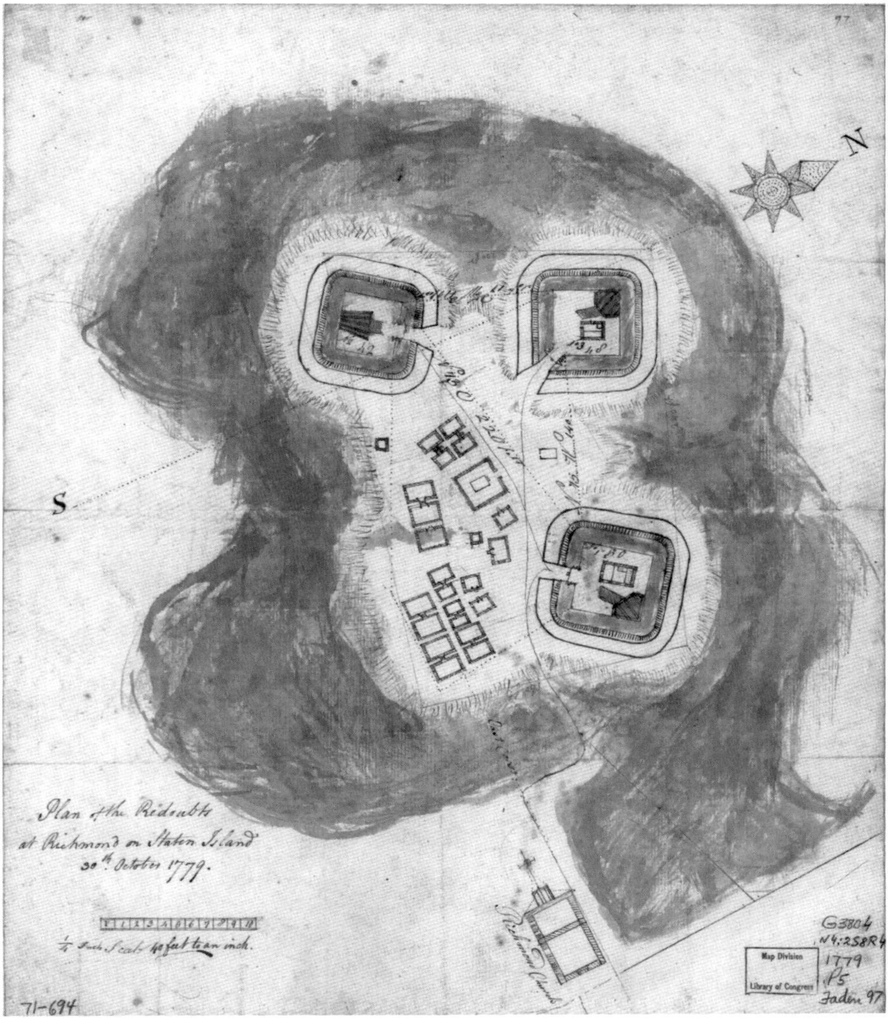

A 1:480 scale plan of the British redoubts and buildings above Richmond. The location of the southwest (*top left*) earthwork is now the elevated second tee at LaTourette Golf Course. *Library of Congress.*

atop the second tee at LaTourette Golf Course and looking downhill at the hole is standing in the same spot Simcoe would have looked out for attackers from the north. The second redoubt was near the first hole, and the third was on the hairpin turn of the golf cart path between the two others. Just southeast on the hillside, the Howe Spring, which provided the camp with fresh water, still bubbles to the surface and flows into Richmond Creek.[567]

The fort was the subject of archaeological examinations published by the New York Historical Society in 1919.[568] Most of the evidence uncovered by the team, like almost all evidence studied by archaeologists, came from rubbish pits found just below the crest of the hill, where the log huts were located. There, they found enough shells and animal bones to conclude that a relatively large number of men had been encamped there throughout the duration of the war. Also proving this was the range of military debris unearthed. It was the custom of the British army to wear numbered uniform buttons signifying their regiment. As such, buttons were logged from many units, including the Fifth, Twenty-Second, Twenty-Third, Thirty-Seventh, Forty-Fourth, Fifty-Fifth and Fifty-Seventh Regiments of Foot; the Forty-Second Royal Highlanders; and the Royal Provincials, as well as pewter buttons of the Hessians.[569]

Clearly, Richmond County was a temporary home for a vast number of British, Hessian and provincial troops throughout the American Revolution. Although they took care to defend themselves, their fortified island in the middle of New York Harbor would be tested many times.

SPIES AND VIGILANTES OF RICHMOND'S UNOFFICIAL WAR

Despite its Tory leanings, British commanders were keenly aware that an island on the front line with dozens of small inlets and kills could easily become an intelligence pipeline for both sides. As such, General Howe and his successors set up strict rules governing the actions of Staten Islanders.

The regulations were firm at the outset and only got more stringent as the war progressed. In 1777, only Cole's Ferry near the Watering Place and Decker's Ferry in Port Richmond were allowed to operate. Then, by 1778, even Decker's was shuttered. Prices were set on wheat, rye, corn, hay and flour, and restrictions on the amount of salt that could be transported were strictly enforced. In 1779, the properties of known rebels were confiscated and used for crops and dairy in the British supply chain, and travel in and out of the county required the permission of General Skinner.[570]

Despite the rules, Continental partisans were able to gather a steady stream of intelligence on Staten Island since the first moment the British arrived, and Staten Islanders would play a significant role in clandestine operations throughout the war.

The most noteworthy of the county's covert operators was the Mersereau spy ring. The Mersereaus were a large Richmond County clan led by their patriarch, Joshua, who owned the second of the county's two shipyards. Unlike his competitor, Richard Lawrence, he was one of the island's most outspoken Whigs. He was assisted in his movements by his son and chief accomplice, John LaGrange Mersereau, and his brothers, John and Jacob.

On the eve of Howe's landing, most of the family fled to New Jersey and formed an underground network under the command of militia colonel Elias Dayton.[571] Their first action took place in August 1776, when a family member who remained on the island, likely John LaGrange, was able to eavesdrop and report the details of a conversation in a British camp discussing how twenty thousand of their troops would soon embark on transports.[572] When Washington realized the value, he instructed Johsua Mersereau to slip John LaGrange back onto the island to continue gathering intelligence there and in Manhattan.[573]

The Mersereaus also completed important operations outside of Staten Island. When Washington retreated across the Delaware in the winter of 1776, just before his famous raid on Trenton, he ordered all of the boats along the river brought to the Pennsylvania shore to prevent Howe's pursuit. It was Joshua Mersereau and his brother John who, after leaving nothing to chance, uncovered a secret cache of Durham boats that were deliberately sunk and concealed in such a way that they could be quickly resurfaced for use.[574] Had they not found them, the British forces might have been able to pursue the rebels into Pennsylvania. The legend of Washington's crossing, and perhaps even the fate of the rebellion, was saved thanks in part to the Staten Island family.[575]

John LaGrange Mersereau operated behind enemy lines on and around Staten Island for approximately eighteen months. At first, he used one of his father's apprentices, John Parker, as a courier between himself and members of the ring in New Jersey. However, after three successful missions, Parker was captured at Amboy, beaten and thrown in jail. John LaGrange took the bold step of visiting him in prison, hoping to supply him with clothes and water, but his condition was grave. Parker died within a day of his capture.[576]

Now forced to be both spy and courier, John LaGrange devised a plan to pass messages to his father by using Shooter's Island off the Mariner's Harbor shoreline. He also made covert visits to him in Elizabeth and, on one attempt, was nearly caught. He was forced to hide in an old New Jersey barn for a full twenty-four hours, and when he managed to return to Staten Island the following night, he was chased by the British garrison.[577]

Sensing that Billop's militiamen were growing suspicious, John LaGrange hung up his spy hat in 1778. Due to a birth deformity, he was unable to hold a musket and was thus unable to join units in the field. Instead, the army sent him (and would later send other Mersereaus) to the barracks at Rutland, Massachusetts, where he served as a deputy commissary of British prisoners captured at Saratoga. After the war, he briefly returned to Staten Island but lived out the bulk of his days in the Southern Tier of Upstate New York. He died in Oswego in 1841 at eighty-three years of age, but not before finally filing for his Revolutionary War pension a year earlier. He was worried about the financial security of his numerous children and died without knowing whether he would receive it. In the end, it was honorably paid to his descendants, declaring that he had "conducted himself in this delicate branch of volunteer duty to the satisfaction of his commanding officer and the advantage of the American cause."[578]

Back on Staten Island, much of the difficult espionage work passed to John LaGrange's sixteen-year-old brother, Jacob. From Jersey, he crossed the kills and hid in a relative's cellar, where another Mersereau, Paul, furnished him with the latest intelligence. Around 1779, the organization of the ring fell on the elder John Mersereau, who operated six spies throughout the region for the remainder of the war. Two of those were likely also Staten Islanders: a LaTourette (the record is unclear whether it was Peter or Paul) and Abraham Banker, who may have gone by the alias Amicus Reipublicae.[579] LaTourette was rumored to be a wood carrier for the British, which allowed him the freedom to travel, and he could correspond with and help plot the escape of captured American officers.[580] He also helped coordinate the efforts of the Fitz Randolphs of Woodbridge, as they led partisan bands that frequently raided British positions, stole supplies and kidnapped officers.[581]

Overall, Richmond County became a center of clandestine activity during the American Revolution, and Washington delighted in the task of using its spy networks. In fact, he was so pleased with the work of the Mersereau ring that he boasted to Congress in 1777, "I keep people constantly on Staten Island, who give me daily information on the operations on the enemy."[582] Just a year into the British occupation, the commander-in-chief ordered Colonel Dayton to send a total of twenty spies to the island.[583]

The British were also eager to cultivate networks that could operate across the kills, though perhaps less successfully. There is evidence that General Knyphausen was duped by faulty intelligence while on the island, and to

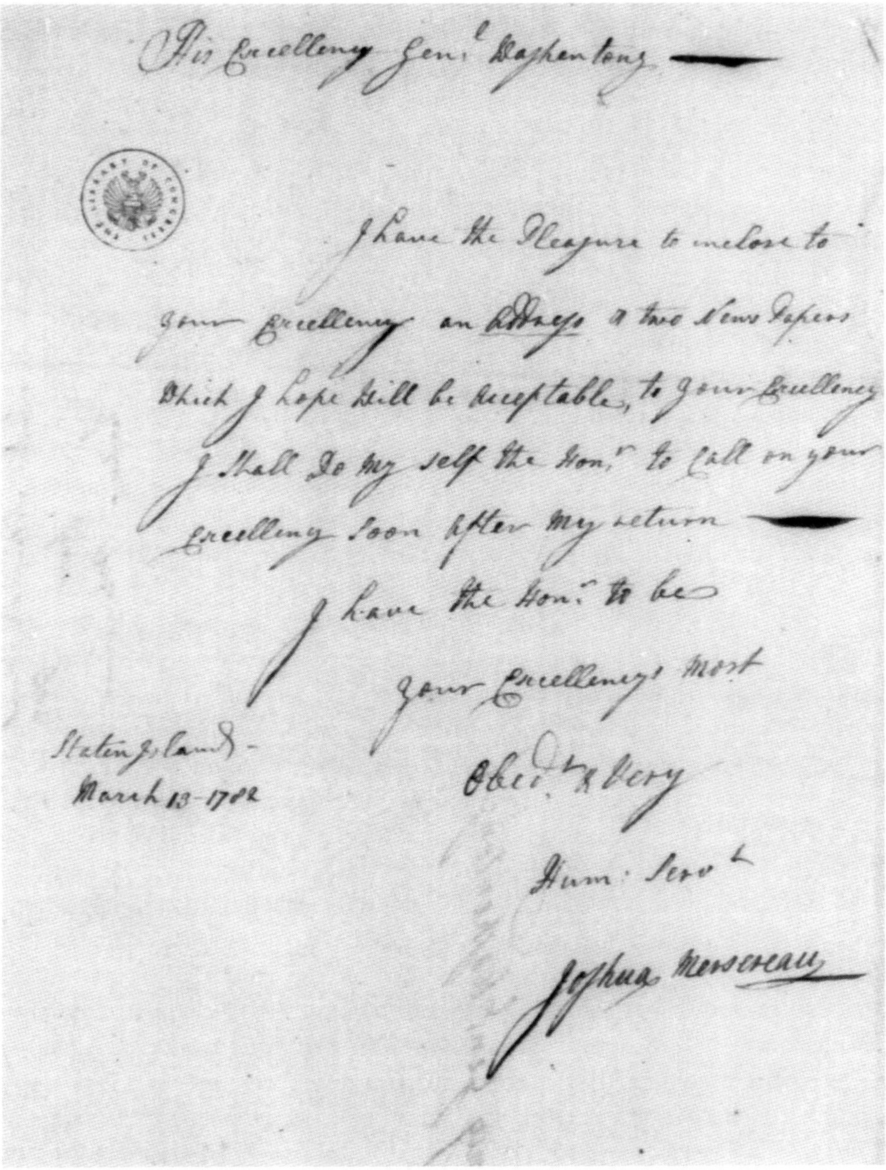

His Excellency Gen.l Washington —

I have the Pleasure to inclose to your Excellency an Address & two News Papers Which I hope Will be acceptable, to your Excellency I Shall Do my self the Hon.r to Call on your Excellency Soon after my return —

I have the Hon.r to be

Your Excellencys most

Obed.t & Very

Hum: Serv.t

Joshua Mersereau

Staten Island —
March 13-1782

Washington was in frequent contact with his spy ring in Richmond County and often received letters like this from Joshua Mersereau, dated March 13, 1782, from Staten Island. *Library of Congress.*

Washington's pleasure, General Skinner fell for John Mersereau's brief sham as a double agent, passing false information on twelve thousand soon-to-arrive French and Spanish soldiers.[584]

In 1777, Britain's most renowned spymaster was lodging on Staten Island, and it is where he wrote his last will and testament. John André, then a captain in the Twenty-Sixth Regiment of Foot and the close acquaintance of Simcoe, was likely residing at the Cucklestowne Inn in Richmond when he prepared the document that bequeathed the bulk of his estate to his brother, William, and three sisters. Due to the partial destruction of the Richmond County Courthouse, it was recorded in New York and probated there after his execution for espionage in his dealings with Benedict Arnold.[585]

For the most part though, Britain's underground war on Staten Island involved partisan bands rather than formal spy rings, and the most complete description of these operations is found in Papas's *That Ever Loyal Island*. Of these bands, the most notorious were the Hatfields, led by Cornelius and John Smith Hatfield, who were originally from Elizabethtown but joined up with Loyalists and British forces on Staten Island in 1778.[586]

Hiding out in Staten Island's many secluded areas, the group was able to strike quickly and violently against Whig communities in New Jersey and known rebel families in the county. By the end of the war, it would earn a reputation as one of the most violent partisan outfits after a series of murders, abductions and rabid plundering. While it often acted as British reconnaissance, and during large engagements was attached to the New Jersey Volunteers, it typically operated outside of the scope of the British command structure and in a gray area of ethical conduct.[587]

A second band on the island was led by Captain Nathaniel Robbins, a British native who settled in the Long Neck area just before the war. It rivaled the Hatfields in terms of brutality against Whigs on Staten Island and across the Kill in Rahway. One contemporary, Raymond Tysen, said, "Robbins was a very brutal man, and several murders, committed on Staten Island, were chargeable to him."[588] The gang operated just a hair above downright banditry, disguising themselves at night to indiscriminately rob and assault travelers on Staten Island's roads.[589]

Still another Tory band that used Staten Island as a base of operations was led by Titus, a former slave who had fled the farm of John Corlies in Colt's Neck after learning of the British army's offer of freedom. Proving himself courageous at the Battle of Monmouth in 1778, he was given the honorary title of Colonel Tye. He led a small band of African American Loyalists on incursions into Monmouth County, where he was familiar with every trail and backwater. His reputation grew as he and his men hunted Whig raiders like John Russell, who organized raids from Monmouth against Staten Island. In fact, it would be a fight at the Colt's Neck home of another Whig partisan leader, Joshua Huddy, also known to raid Staten Island, where Titus and many of his men met their demise.[590]

It was this type of internecine warfare, more similar to a civil war or a blood feud between families, that took the heaviest toll on Staten Islanders. This was especially true later in the war as fewer major campaigns occupied the attention of the soldiers in the field. As Raymond Tysen recalled, "Organized bands of Tories then prowled about, robbing friend and foe; and it was no uncommon thing, during a scene of dreadful violence, for a man to discover that he was pillaged by his nearest relation."[591]

The majority of smaller engagements that occurred on Staten Island were typically the result of incursions by nearby Whig bands, which oftentimes comprised former islanders now seeking refuge in New Jersey. Given the heavy British presence, most of these quick raids took place under the cover of darkness, and often, their goals were microstrategic, attempting to hit a particular person or property. The Dawson family farm along the Kill Van Kull, the storehouse owned by John Bedell near Richmond and, of course, the Billop property were all frequent targets of nighttime forays. In one incident, club-wielding Whigs broke into the home of Peter Houseman and killed him instantly, and his son-in-law, John Tysen, barely survived. In another brutal encounter, the home of John Bodine was raided for its valuables, but after finding nothing, they tortured him with a hot iron in front of his family until a nearby British patrol fired a warning shot.[592]

One of the leading Whig bands was the Fitz Randolphs. Originally led by Captain Nathaniel Fitz Randolph, the group often crossed the kills on whaleboats, muffling the sounds of the oars with leather as they went deep into Fresh Kills and other inlets. After his death in combat at Elizabethtown, Fitz Randolph's cousin Asher Fitz Randolph took his place. The band also played an active role in assisting the operations of the Mersereaus.[593]

Captain Baker Hendricks, also from Elizabethtown, was commissioned as a privateer and led two armed whaleboats, the *Flying Squirrel* and *Charming Betsey*, against the Staten Island coast and Tory shipping along the kills. So brutal were his actions that New Jersey governor Livingston revoked his commission after particularly depraved attacks on civilians later in the war.[594]

Other privateering raiders operated during the 1780s in Raritan Bay and the Raritan River. Captain Adam Hyler was perhaps the most prolific of Whig whaleboat captains in the region, leading successful raids against the South Shore, including one occasion during which he captured a British vessel in Prince's Bay in 1782.[595] For many years, he and his men were the most dominant brown-water naval force in the inland waterways between Staten Island and Little Egg Harbor.

6

THE BATTLES FOR STATEN ISLAND

Throughout its seven years of occupation by British and Hessian troops, Staten Island was the site of several engagements, which, while small compared to the major battles of the Revolution, did occasionally involve thousands of regular troops and were part of the broader strategic operations of the opposing armies. Regardless of their size and importance to the overall war narrative, no sketch of Staten Island's history would be complete without a summary of the actions taken there during the struggle for American independence. For modern residents of Staten Island, its Revolutionary War history may become more interesting as they realize their neighborhoods were the sites of numerous engagements. The following is a chronological look at these events.

1776

In the fall of 1776, the war in the New York theater was centered on northern Manhattan, yet in the same week Washington elected to abandon Harlem Heights for White Plains,[596] the rebels were making a small-scale diversionary offensive on Staten Island. The attack was ordered by Brigadier General Hugh Mercer, a professional soldier whose first taste of combat against the British government came at the Battle of Culloden in April 1746, while serving in the Jacobite army of Bonnie Prince Charlie.[597]

Just months after leading an attack on Richmond Town, General Hugh Mercer was killed at the Battle of Princeton, becoming an early hero of the American cause. *New York Public Library.*

Thirty years later, on the night of October 15, Mercer and Colonel Jacob Griffin led a detachment of rebel soldiers in a dawn attack on the Watering Place.[598] However, after marching to Richmond Town, they came on three companies of British, Hessian and Provincial troops who were previously alerted to the impending incursion. Heading a battalion of infantry and a company of riflemen, Griffin tried to flank the town from the east, while a second division approached the town along the main road along Fresh Kills. Both columns arrived before daybreak but not before the bulk of the enemy had time to flee. Gunfire was exchanged between the British and Griffin's unit as he pushed into the town, and the colonel himself was wounded in the foot. The rebels took a number of prisoners from inside St. Andrew's Church, which was likely being used as an infirmary. But as British reinforcements approached from the north, they were forced to quickly retreat across the Blazing Star ferry.[599]

Three of the prisoners (two Hessian and one British from the Fourteenth Regiment) were able to provide Mercer with intelligence that he relayed to Washington on the number of troops on Staten Island and the size of Hessian reinforcements soon expected from Europe.[600]

Despite this small success at Richmond Town, the remainder of the year would prove disastrous overall for the rebels, as the British would quickly pursue the main body of troops through central New Jersey and across the Delaware (thankfully, Mersereau discovered the few remaining boats). Mercer made the crossing with Washington on Christmas Eve but was mortally wounded while leading the vanguard at the Battle of Princeton on January 2, 1777. After his horse was shot from under him, he refused to surrender and was bayonetted,[601] a final action that made him an early hero of the Revolution.

1777 and the "Battle" of Staten Island

After the famous battles at Trenton and Princeton, Washington's troops tangled with British forces in smaller engagements throughout central Jersey as Howe endeavored to take Philadelphia by land. As a result, Staten Island was used as both a point of embarkation for the main body of British brigades on Howe's campaign and a constant base for small raids into rebel-held territory.

In February, a detachment of approximately two hundred soldiers set out from Cole's Ferry near the Watering Place for a surprise attack behind the enemy lines at Sandy Hook. They entered the Neversink inlet and landed on the beach about two miles below the enemy's position. The rebels were caught off guard and quickly retreated to the hills of the Atlantic Highlands but not before several were killed and seventy-four were captured.[602] Later that month, and again in March, two smaller raids from Staten Island to Elizabethtown and Rahway netted nothing more than a few head of cattle.[603]

In June, Howe decided to make his move against Philadelphia. First, he consolidated and staged his troops on Staten Island, at Amboy and at their farthest outpost along the Raritan River at Brunswick. From there, he could either strike west to reach Philadelphia through central Jersey or feint a land movement and quickly return his men down the river to embark on transports in Raritan Bay for an attack by sea.[604]

On June 11, a day of extraordinary heat, Private Döhla and his company were ordered to march from the Watering Place "24 English miles" to Amboy. Along the way, he records that "two Ansbach grenadiers fell dead from exhaustion and were buried on the spot immediately."[605] Arriving in town by nightfall, his unit was forced to sleep under the stars in Amboy's cemetery.[606]

In another account, a twenty-two-year-old Beyrouth infantryman, Stephen Popp, also recounted the long march and said, when his company made Amboy on the morning of June 12, all "were looking hopelessly wasted and neglected."[607]

For a few weeks, the armies played a game of cat and mouse before an engagement at Metuchen between 2,500 men under Lord Stirling and two columns of British and Hessians under Cornwallis and Vaughan. By the end of June, Howe ordered a full withdrawal to Staten Island to begin the embarkation process for a sea attack up the Delaware to land near Philadelphia.[608] The shoreline of Staten Island was very much alive during the period, as Major Andre's journal notes that it took three full days for the 11,000 troops and hundreds of horses, wagons and artillery to cross between Amboy and Billop's ferry.[609] He also noted that in their haste to board the large transports, six regiments stood waiting at Prince's Bay for their transports to arrive but were then forced to march once again, because of this "misunderstanding," to the Watering Place where they actually stood waiting.[610]

On July 23, Howe and the main body of the British army passed out of sight around Sandy Hook on their way to Chesapeake Bay, where they would march from the south to take Philadelphia. He left Knyphausen[611] and was temporarily back on Staten Island with approximately three thousand soldiers.[612] The general positioned the Fifty-Second and Second Hessian Regiments in a series of camps from his headquarters at the Watering Place south along the coast to the Narrows. Skinner's brigade manned the defenses on the west and south shores,[613] and the Rangers occupied Richmond.[614]

Times were tense on the island as the narrow waters between it and New Jersey served as the only barrier between the two armies. On August 7, Private Döhla was awoken at midnight and his unit was ordered to set off in pursuit of some rebels who crossed over, most likely to probe the defenses.[615] Other troops fought in a brief skirmish that night before the Americans retreated. A week later, on August 19, Lieutenant Colonel Edward Vaughan Dongan of Skinner's New Jersey Volunteers, a twenty-nine-year-old descendant of the former governor,[616] led a similar retaliatory raid twenty-seven miles into the interior of New Jersey, returning with fourteen prisoners and seventy head of cattle.[617]

Hoping to strike a quick counterattack, General Sullivan ordered two brigades to attack British positions on Staten Island. At 2:00 a.m. on the morning of August 22,[618] the rebels began crossing the kills for what would later be referred to as the Battle of Staten Island. Fortunately, several accounts of this engagement survive from both sides, ranging from the diaries of American captain Andrew Lee to the papers of Stephen Kemble, the deputy adjutant-general under Generals Howe, Clinton and Gage.[619] There is a sketched map and diagram of the troop movements by Major Thomas Millidge of the Jersey Volunteers. Additionally, there is a legal record of the court-martial proceedings against General Sullivan for his actions during the foray, of which he was eventually acquitted on all counts.

Armed with some intelligence of the enemy's positions, Sullivan divided his total force of two thousand men into two brigades. One was placed under the command of General Preudhomme de Borre, which Sullivan would also personally accompany. It was assigned to land at the New Blazing Star Ferry

Left: General John Sullivan led over two thousand men in a raid on Staten Island on August 22, 1777, against three thousand men under General Knyphausen. *New York Public Library.*

Right: Baron Wilhelm von Knyphausen commanded British and Hessian units on Staten Island in 1777 during Sullivan's raid. *New York Public Library.*

(Travis), cross over the marshy fields and outflank a regiment of the New Jersey Volunteers under Colonel Barton, who was posted along the coast. The second brigade was under the command of General Smallwood. It landed closer to Elizabethtown point and immediately attacked an outpost. Smallwood then sent a detachment toward Decker's Ferry to surprise a regiment of Skinner's Brigade that camped there.[620]

Owing to the poor advice of a local guide, the initial attack on Decker's Ferry did not go according to plan. Instead of sneaking to the rear of the British fortifications, they "were exposed to the full view of the enemy" and were able to only destroy several boats and storehouses before being driven off by a gathering force.[621] Smallwood's main column and the detachment then set off south on the road to Richmond (taking modern Richmond Avenue from Port Richmond to New Springville), where they believed the enemy was gathering and where, according to the plan, they would rendezvous with de Borre's column. Taking Richmond was the main objective not only because it was the county seat but also because it was the point where the entire body of rebel troops could easily ford Fresh Kills and Richmond Creek and loop around back to the Old Blazing Star Ferry (Rossville), where they would retreat back across to New Jersey.[622]

The main camp of Hessian regulars at the Watering Place was stirred early in the morning from the report of musketry on the opposite end of the island. "We received a strong visit here on Staten Island from the rebels," remembered Private Döhla.[623] In minutes, his unit was marching quickly to Richmond under the command of General John Campbell,[624] commander of the Fifty-Seventh Regiment of Foot, who happened to be visiting the island and reviewing the troops the day before.[625]

At the same time, around sunrise, de Borre's brigade also divided in two. A detachment under Colonel Matthias Ogden rowed up into the Kills to surround a small company of men at a sentry post where the main branch of Fresh Kills splits with Richmond Creek just east of the modern Route 440 bridge.[626] Ogden, with about five hundred men, "completely surprised the Enemy, killed a few" and took several prisoners.[627] The rest retreated southeast and were soon pursued. Ogden next attacked the outpost farther up the creek commanded by Lieutenant Colonel Dongan (either at an outpost near Greenridge or farther east near Giffords Lane), quickly routing the enemy with musketry and hand-to-hand combat.

Most of Skinner's Brigade fled south toward the entrenchments at Prince's Bay, but in the exchange, Lieutenant Colonel Dongan was shot.[628] The *New York Gazette* published an account of the incident, calling him an officer of distinguished bravery and reporting, "Gentlemen of uncommon Merit, both as a Man and Soldier, is since dead of his wounds….He was in his 39th Year, and has left a young distressed Widow to lament the Death of an affectionate Husband. Their only Child died a few Hours before him."[629]

Ogden correctly sensed that reinforcements would soon come but overestimated the distance between his unit and the main columns. He marched with his prisoners back to the Old Blazing Star, where after waiting a bit as a precaution, he began to cross.[630]

Not far away, on the northern side of the Fresh Kills, de Borre and Sullivan marched about two miles inland across the marsh, according to the plan, before turning right along the road now known as Victory Boulevard to attack the New Blazing Star.[631] There they surprised Colonel Barton, who had his men "paraded in a cornfield."[632] The rebels tried to flank them on their right, and after each side exchanged a fierce fusillade, they managed to kill "about 5, & made near 30 Prisoners,"[633] including Barton himself. The survivors of the attack were forced to swim across Fresh Kills to the southern half of the island, while de Borre and Sullivan doubled back to meet Smallwood's column on the road to Richmond.

General Sullivan, atop his horse as the column marched along the road near New Springville, called out to his men: "Now my lads we will have some fun, the enemy are advancing and we must give them a drubbing."[634] Unfortunately, the initial success wouldn't last. At Richmond, Skinner's Brigade was quickly reinforced by Hessians who occupied the commanding heights of the fort. A frontal attack against Campbell's full force was out of the question. Instead, Sullivan hastily crossed the Richmond Creek, avoided the town and marched for the Old Blazing Star.[635] Seeing the rebels moving rapidly toward the shoreline, Campbell, Skinner and the Hessians set off in pursuit.

The British forces kept their main units toward the south (perhaps along modern Amboy Road) in an attempt to reach their flank as the rebels retreated along the Kills toward the ferry (along modern Arthur Kill Road).[636] The fatigue some of Sullivan's troops faced and the desire of others to plunder caused the column to be spread extensively along the road between Richmond and the Old Blazing Star.[637]

At the ferry, a chaotic embarkation ensued. Some of the witnesses at Sullivan's court-martial attributed this to his poor planning, while others claimed that his order to bring up additional boats was ignored. Nonetheless, the few boats Ogden had used the night before would be their only source of egress. To protect their retreat, the general ordered a picket line posted at the heights above the ferry near the Blazing Star cemetery.[638]

At approximately 5:00 p.m., with most of the men safely across, a wagon was sent back toward Richmond to pick up any wounded or stragglers left behind. It didn't get more than half a mile in that direction before those inside sighted the vanguard of an attacking enemy force. The picket of about one hundred men was left in the command of a Captain Carlisle, while reinforcements were sought from the retreating boats. Sullivan ordered a regiment of Maryland Militia to form along a fence line to the right of the picket, and a skirmish ensued.[639] Captain Andrew Lee recorded the fight in his diary:

> *The fire now began general from left to right at the distance of about 90 yards, for the space of half an hour, in the course of which time the enemy were more than once broke. They endeavored continually to force our front, but finding it impossible they extended their lines beyond our right, and doubling in at the same time, pressing on in front with two pieces of artillery*

> *forced us from our fence, and finding it impossible to hold out against five times our numbers with the advantage of artillery, it was thought advisable to surrender. Our loss in killed was incredible, not exceeding five men.*[640]

Those who did not surrender with Captain Lee fled as the British charged with bayonets. Now occupying the heights, Campbell's "artillery fired several rounds of Grape Shot into them as they were Crossing, they were heard to make a great outcry and some of them seen to Jump over board."[641] The battle ended as a British tactical victory, although of no strategic significance. In days, the entire focus of the American army, including Sullivan's Brigade, would turn its attention toward defending Philadelphia from Howe. The estimates of each side's losses vary, ranging from just six to one hundred British killed and ten to fifteen Americans. Most accounts agree that each side took more than one hundred prisoners.[642]

Twenty days later, General Clinton took two companies of Hessian grenadiers, including Private Döhla; three regiments of British infantry; and three hundred men of Skinner's Brigade on a counterattack across the Kills to Elizabethtown to forage for cattle and other provisions. According to Döhla, "The enemy General Putnam appeared with a corps of three thousand Jersey and New England Militiamen and two regular battalions and took an advantageous post....All the following day there was heavy small-arms and cannon fire."[643] Putnam eventually retreated, and the British forces advanced on Newark, which Döhla called "an unimportant place."[644] The army advanced north and engaged the enemy once more at Second River, in modern Belleville, before Clinton decided they had enough beef and headed back to Staten Island.[645] Döhla was happy with the mission's success and remembered that "each private in this detachment, even the servants, received a Spanish dollar as a bonus." However, he also noted that his close friends Privates Johann Cärner and Johann Stöhr died at the Hessian field hospital at the Watering Place.[646]

As this was going on, the bulk of the American operations were elsewhere. Clinton was foraging through New Jersey, and Washington was fighting the Battle of Brandywine near Philadelphia—all as news was trickling in of a looming engagement between Generals Gates and Burgoyne at Saratoga. Despite the shift of the war's focus away from Staten Island, there were several more attempts to raid it throughout the rest of 1777. On at least two occasions that November, attacks came from Elizabethtown, and Skinner's men were able to repel the Continentals after short exchanges of gunfire.[647] The stalemate along the Kills would continue as the war pressed on.

1778

The year 1778 would be marked by efforts on both sides of the sound, as the Kills were then often called, to curtail the amount of illegal smuggling and clandestine information to cross between the lines. Early that winter, General Clinton named Alexander Gardiner wharf officer of Staten Island and ordered any and all goods arriving at the shores land exclusively at Cole's Ferry under the close watch of the main camps.[648]

As the French entered the war on the side of the Americans, 1778 brought a renewed focus on fortifying the island from potential amphibious attacks. In July, Montresor began major work on the earthworks of the Narrows, while General Clinton assigned additional regiments to guard the approaches to the city.[649] Tory newspapers reported almost daily on the fifteen-ship fleet under the Comte d'Estaing, which they said "stood in directly for [Sandy] Hook, and was not more than two miles from the Light-House." The flotilla included the ninety-four-gun *Languedoc*, one of the largest ships afloat.[650] By July 13, the French were scouting the harbor and sounding the channel, seemingly making preparations to sail into New York Bay.[651] However, after probing the defenses of Sandy Hook and of the Narrows and staring down an array of British ships of the line, d'Estaing thought it best to sail around Long Island to make his attack on Rhode Island.

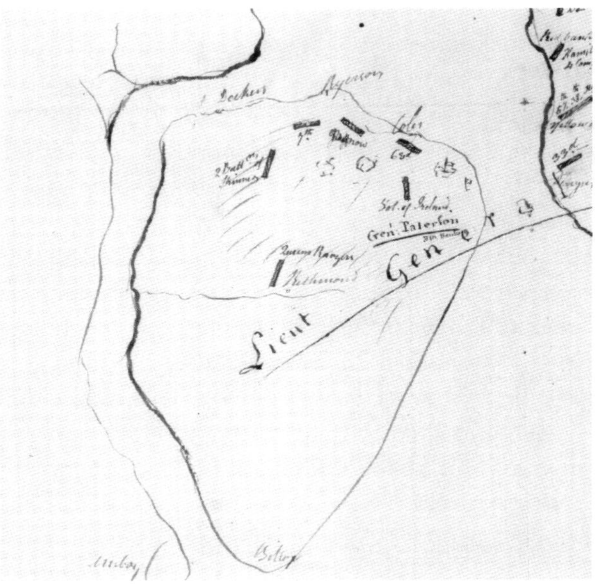

A sketching in the handwriting of Major John André, showing the disposition of troops in 1778, including the Queen's Rangers at Richmond and the Sons of Ireland at the Narrows. *William L. Clements Library, University of Michigan.*

General Clinton was on Staten Island for a prisoner exchange on July 22, when from the heights, he saw the French fleet weigh anchor and sail eastward out of sight.[652] Of the prisoners who were exchanged that day, missing among them was Christopher Billop, who was captured for the first time just weeks earlier on June 5. "But O Ye destructive, butchering, British monsters, beware!" said the Whig paper the *New Jersey Gazette*. "Last night Capt. Nathaniel Fitz Randolph of Woodbridge, with a party of 15 volunteers, landed on Staten Island, surprised and made prisoners 13 of the militia of the island who were on guard; also Col. Christopher Billop."[653] Remembering the story years later, an eyewitness recalled that the colonel was a guest at a ball at the home of the Disosway family near Rossville. Unknown to their neighbors at the time, the Disosways were secretly Whig partisans and were somehow able to alert Fitz Randolph of Billop's attendance. The Jersey brigand and Fitz Randolph's crew managed to surprise Billop's party on its way home as they stumbled along the road in the wee hours of the morning.[654] Colonel Billop was taken first to Woodbridge and then to a jail near Morristown, where he would remain for nearly nine months.[655]

1779

The winter of 1778–79 was especially cold, and as the temperature dropped, the demand for wood for the men cramped in small huts throughout British camps in the region rose. It quickly rose on the priority list of Henry Clinton. The general issued new provisions to supply the men from Richmond County by confiscating more properties from known Whigs and ordered the continued clearing of the island.[656]

New Jersey rebels undoubtedly received some intelligence of the desperate need for wood and the planned source of new supplies, and a plot was hatched to raid Prince's Bay and capture or destroy the barges carrying Clinton's cordwood. The action started off according to plan, and the raiders were able to seize one of the boats at the outset. However, either the company of Skinner's Brigade or a detachment of the Queen's Rangers was posted there on guard duty, and as the raiders approached the sandy beach, they "kept up such a brisk fire upon them that they were obliged to relinquish their prize which had been aground, and made the best of the way home."[657]

In the fighting, the *New York Gazette* noted that a Staten Islander named Mr. Sleight did "receive a wound in his breast."[658] It can be surmised that he survived, as this Mr. Sleight was likely Cornelius Slaght, whose family lived near the Old Blazing Star and may have used the Dutch spelling of their name among their Staten Island neighbors. The records of the county supervisors note a payment of one pound and nine shillings to a doctor for "three visits to Cornelius Slaght and Dressing his wounds."[659] If so, he survived until at least 1820, when the census records him as still living in the area along with his eight children and one slave.[660] The Sleight family burial ground in Rossville, also called the Old Blazing Star Cemetery, and the Bethel Methodist Church Cemetery in Tottenville are well-populated with his descendants.

In same March 22, 1779 issue of the *New York Gazette*, there is also a mention of "two or three Different parties of [rebels] that have been lately at the Seat of Col. Christopher Billop of the same island, in order to captivate him once more, with a view to get him for an Exchange."[661] This means that almost as soon as Billop was paroled, the Whigs were keeping a watchful eye on his estate and making attempts to capture him as a chip in negotiations.

On June 23, just over a year from his first capture, the rebels were successful in capturing him once again. For weeks, Whig lookouts perched in the belfry of St. Peter's Church in Perth Amboy (adjacent to the present 1852 structure still visible from Tottenville)[662] before finally spying him strolling the grounds of his estate. That night, a party of five men led by David Coddington, a relative of the Fitz Randolphs, and including Staten Islander Peter LaTourette, rowed silently across the bay with muffled oars. From a slave, they learned the password the picket guards were using and were able to approach the house without causing alarm. They broke into Billop's home, walked past the room where less than three years earlier the fate of the war was discussed, climbed the stairs and seized him in his bed. Coddington quickly rowed him back to New Jersey just as Billop's own men were coming to his rescue.[663] The Tory account in the *Royal Gazette* was less kind about the kidnappers, claiming they "abused him and his family, and most inhumanely attempted to bayonet his wife and his children....They kicked him before them to the boat, and wounded him with their bayonets, behaving in every respect like a parcel of inhuman savages."[664]

Regardless of whether or not his family suffered these depredations, Billop's own six months in Burlington jail were not pleasant, even according to New Jersey's Whig commissioner of prisons. He was shackled at the wrists and ankles and fed a diet of only bread and water, allegedly as a reprisal for the treatment of two recently captured American officers. As Elias Boudinot, a delegate to the Continental Congress and Commissary of Prisons, informed Billop, "It seems nothing short of retaliation will teach Britons to act like men of humanity."[665] As difficult as his confinement may have been, at the very least, he wouldn't suffer it alone for very long.

On receiving intelligence that the rebels were transporting a supply of small boats over land near Somerset Courthouse, Lieutenant Colonel Simcoe led the Queen's Rangers and the Bucks County Volunteers in pursuit. They departed Staten Island and landed at Amboy on October 26, 1779. The plan was well thought out and, for the most part, went as hoped. Simcoe set off with his cavalry after the caravan of boats, while the infantry laid a trap. The Bucks County men were ordered to guard the bridge over the Raritan connecting Sommerset and South Amboy, in the hope that the rebels would pursue the cavalry to the spot where they were likely to ferry back across to the island.[666]

Simcoe and his men quickly found the column of boats, burning eighteen of them along with their carriages, and continued on a path of destruction through surrounding countryside. He burst open a Whig jail, freeing three Tory prisoners and taking several of his own.[667] As his dragoons made their way back toward Amboy, near Brunswick, they came under fire from a rebel militia company that concealed itself behind some downed trees. Simcoe's horse was shot from under him, and he was knocked unconscious in the fall. His last recollection was hearing the words "Now, now!"[668] Believing him dead, Captain Parker took command and charged the militiamen several times, killing several before they fled in retreat. The Rangers returned to Staten Island the following morning, losing just four men in the raid after leaving a seventy-mile trail of burnt stores and harassed citizens in the heart of enemy territory. Simcoe woke up a prisoner.[669]

On November 9, he was removed from his temporary confinement and sent to jail in Burlington, where he was placed in proximity to his friend Christopher Billop, who was still chained and shackled. He immediately sent correspondence to Governor Livingston of New Jersey, General Clinton and even Washington to negotiate a prisoner exchange for the two of them.[670] Simcoe also advocated for other prisoners suffering equal, if not worse, depredations. Two private soldiers, held without provisions as "their emaciated appearance fully confirmed," were transferred from Burlington after Simcoe's negotiations with the local sheriff.[671]

His efforts toward securing an exchange finally paid off at the end of December, and the *New York Gazette* reported that Washington personally approved the exchange for both him and Billop at the same time.[672] On New Year's Eve, Simcoe rejoined his unit at the fort overlooking Richmond Town and was pleased with what his second-in-command, Major Armstrong, had done to "render their post both comfortable and defensible," for as he noted, "they soon found the advantages of their very extraordinary labors."[673]

1780

The day Simcoe went back across the Arthur Kill was the last day it was navigable before freezing over in what was then called the Hard Winter. Lord Stirling, then camped with a large body of the Continental army at Morristown, decided to use the frozen Kill Van Kull and the unprecedented heavy snow to his advantage in a surprise attack on Skinner's Brigade. He received permission from Washington to launch his raid on Staten Island with the goal of securing much-needed food and supplies that could be brought back with relative ease by sled.[674]

Stirling and his 2,500 men departed from Elizabethtown late at night on January 14 and landed in the vicinity of Morningstar Road. The main column marched east toward the entrenchments at the Watering Place, while a second detachment passed through Dongan Hills for an approach on the fortifications at the Narrows.[675] Unfortunately, the British commanders, including Simcoe and Colonel Abraham Van Buskirk of the New Jersey Volunteers,[676] had received early intelligence of the attack, and when the sun rose, they were primed to defend their positions with 1,800 eager soldiers.

Private Joseph Plumb Martin was part of Stirling's brigade. His account of the Revolution is one of the most widely read, as he seemed to be present for so many of its most dramatic moments. "When we arrived we found Johnny Bull prepared for our reception," he wrote. "To take their works by storm looked too hazardous; to besiege them in regular form was out of the question."[677] A stalemate ensued throughout the day, with the two armies standing in full view of each other from atop adjacent hills. Their positions were identified on a contemporary map that survived in the papers of Henry Clinton. Buskirk occupied the fort at the Watering Place, while the Fifty-Seventh Regiment of Foot and the Hessian Regiment of Bunau moved out from the Fort Hill entrenchments and formed on the heights of New Brighton, likely along present-day Highview Avenue. While on the opposite hill to the southwest, Stirling brought his infantry and artillery to the top of

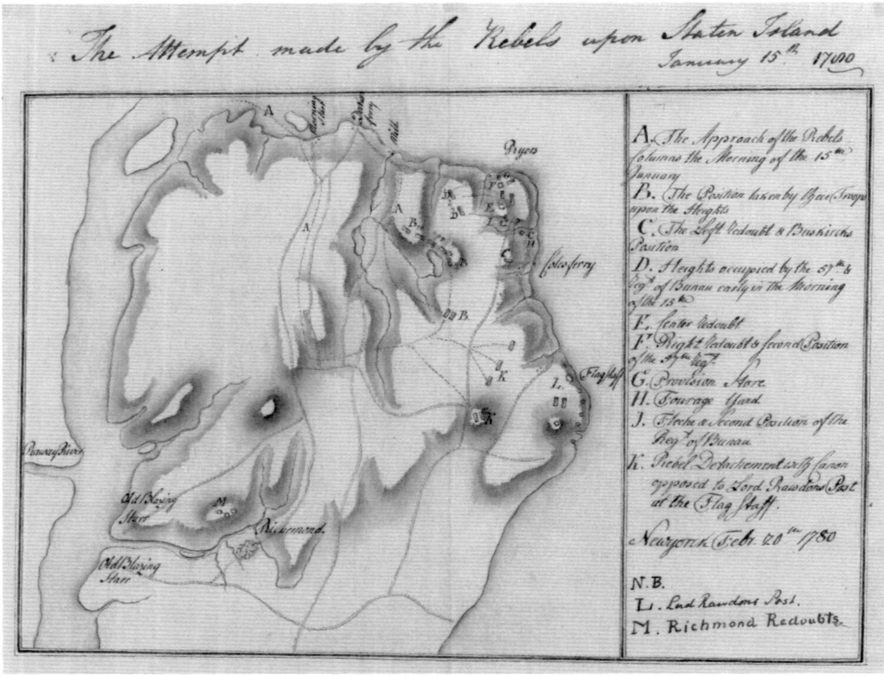

A diagram by Hessian engineer Reinhard Jacob Martin of the engagement of January 15, 1780, when Sullivan and 2,500 men crossed the frozen Kill van Kull. *William L. Clements Library, University of Michigan.*

Grymes Hill, near modern Howard Avenue and the intersection of Forest Avenue and Victory Boulevard. Farther south, a rebel detachment and some field pieces were brought to the property now known as Mount Manresa, with a commanding view over Lord Rawdon and the Volunteers of Ireland guarding the Narrows.[678]

The only artillery fire exchanged that day occurred between a field piece that was dragged over to position above Decker's Ferry and the brig *Hawk*, which was at anchor and locked in ice in the Kill. A detachment under Colonel Willet attacked the small garrison stationed at the Decker house, burning it along with some small boats, and would have continued foraging and burning adjacent buildings had the *Hawk* not opened up with its bow gun.[679] According to one sailor, "We fired on them, shot one Man's Arm off; he bled to death and now lays in the snow; our Firing made them retreat as fast as possible up the Hill to their main Body."[680]

With the mass of rebel troops still arrayed on the heights, the British and Hessian regular infantry perceived their enemy's advantageous position and pulled back toward the Fort Hill redoubts. In doing so, they allowed the rebels to cut off the main roads of communication between their encampment and the Queen's Rangers stationed at Richmond.[681]

Simcoe prepared the fort for battle, which, to his chagrin, did not come. The cannon of the three redoubts were positioned to fire at the pathways through which the rebels would likely approach, and stacks of small stones were placed at those points to cause a shrapnel effect should a round of shot make contact. Simcoe's men drove spiked nails through boards and covered them in the snow along the paths most easily accessible, and for good measure, the first redoubt was set up in a way that allowed it to be abandoned and left to the enemy, luring them directly into a crossfire trap.[682]

By midday, the Queen's Rangers had captured some deserters, who informed Simcoe that the Continental officers thought it was not worthwhile to assault Richmond, as they "were sure of obstinate resistance."[683] It's clear that they had some intelligence of the defenses and believed that the town and fort could be more easily stormed from the rear with the full force of the brigade after the engagements at the Watering Place and Narrows. Surprisingly, word soon came from Lord Rawdon that Stirling's men did not advance or fire at either redoubt. Simcoe hoped to attack the enemy's rear while, he assumed, they waited for more field pieces. He asked Billop to assemble his men at Richmond, but neither the colonel's entreaties nor Simcoe's could get a large enough body of men for the attack. "They assembled to drink at various public houses, and to hear news, or were busy in providing for the temporary security of their cattle and effects."[684]

Simcoe was forced to lay aside his plans both because of a lack of men and as a result of the depth of the snow, which would have made sending out any advance patrols of cavalry impossible. In the end, the Queen's Rangers would man the fort above Richmond that night, assuming that, as in the past, the Continentals would retreat toward either of the Blazing Star ferries.[685]

Five miles away, on Grymes Hill, Joseph Plumb Martin and his company were suffering intolerably. They spent the night "upon a bare bleak hill, in full rake of the northwest wind, with no other covering or shelter than the canopy of the heavens, and no fuel but some old rotten rails which we dug up through the snow, which was two or three feet deep; the weather was cold enough to cut a man in two."[686]

Overnight, General Knyphausen sent a small number of vessels from New York City carrying fresh troops, and when morning finally broke, Stirling saw no opportunity to engage in a successful siege of the fortifications.[687]

What the Americans had not realized was that the ice around the Staten Island shoreline was, in fact, too packed frozen to land, so the reinforcements were essentially putting on a spectacle from their boats.[688] Nonetheless, the retreat began.

Simcoe set off at dawn with a flanking party of cavalry to cut them off as they attempted to cross back over the Kills.[689] He was too late, but a detachment of the Provincial Cavalry and Seventeenth Dragoons were able to engage the Continental rear guard under Major Edwards, who fended them off long enough to destroy a bridge over the creek at Decker's Ferry. This act prevented the enemy's infantry from pursuing any farther. Edwards lost three men in the fight and killed one of the dragoons.[690]

Whatever the goals of the incursion were, the rebels did manage to get in their fair share of looting. Much of it was done by partisan civilians from Elizabethtown who seized the opportunity to cross the Kills under the relative safety of the American column and raid the homes of their enemies. According to Stirling, a "very inconsiderable part" of the troops also engaged in this behavior, and it was necessary for the general to search each man for stolen items as he returned to Elizabethtown. Each piece of property was catalogued and handed over to Reverend Dr. Caldwell of New Jersey, who volunteered to return every item to its rightful owner.[691]

The looting by Continental regulars did, however, embarrass Washington, and it provided the justification for retaliatory raids into New Jersey for the next several months, in which brutality and pilfering were more of the goal than gaining any strategic advantage.[692]

On January 25, guided by Cornelius Hatfield, Skinner's men made simultaneous attacks on Newark and Elizabethtown, capturing several prisoners at the former and burning the latter's Presbyterian church, courthouse and school. They also took captive a Lieutenant Winant, along with forty-seven of his men.[693]

Weeks later, Skinner's men returned to Elizabethtown, while the Queen's Rangers embarked on a raid from the Old Blazing Star on Woodbridge.[694] Simcoe and two hundred infantrymen crossed the ice around midday, leaving Major Armstrong and a detachment of infantry and artillery at the heights above the Old Blazing Star to cover their retreat. This was one part of a larger plan ordered by General Knyphausen to send a large body of cavalry from New York deep into Bergen County toward Morristown, and the Hussars of the Queen's Rangers had already been deployed for that attack. Simcoe's mission was to create a diversion with his infantry that afternoon.[695]

Finding no one guarding Woodbridge, he "was anxious to fulfill the spirit of his orders" and ventured inland to the road running between Amboy and Elizabethtown. At the crossroads, his column was engaged by a sentinel post, which, in line with Simcoe's desires, sounded the "bugle-horns, drums, and bagpipes"[696] to raise the alarm. After one soldier was killed by "a chance shot of the sentinels," the Queen's Rangers marched back through the snow toward Woodbridge, crossed Woodbridge Creek and then finally went toward the shorefront—all while the rebels stalked them from the rear. Perceiving that the Americans would likely try to occupy the ferry houses on the Jersey side to give them cover as they fired on the Rangers as they delicately crossed the ice, Major Armstrong had them positioned in sight of his guns. At just under one thousand yards, they were well within range. Simcoe also ordered an advanced detachment to covertly set up an ambush just south of the Blazing Star at the point where they intended to walk across. As Simcoe's men ventured over the frozen Arthur Kill, some of the rebels began firing from the ferry house while others pursued from their rear, just as expected. In the resulting fusillade, many rebels were killed along the shoreline before ultimately falling back, while Simcoe's raiding party returned to Richmond with just the one loss.[697]

Two more small raids occurred in March and April, with the net effect of tormenting the sentinels on the opposite shore. Joseph Plumb Martin spent that winter and spring camped at Westfield, rotating every two days to guard duty at Woodbridge and Elizabethtown, and all the while, he noted, "We had next to nothing to eat."[698] His diary records three incursions while he was on duty, including one in which his friend Twist was killed after firing his musket to alert the rest of the company. "I could not restrain my tears, when I saw him next day, with his breast like a sieve, caused by the wounds. He lost his own life by endeavoring to save the lives of others."[699]

After nearly six months of these petty attacks, and bolstered by news that General Clinton captured Charleston (a short campaign in which Simcoe and the Queen's Rangers participated) and on intelligence that Washington's army at Morristown had withered down considerably to under four thousand troops, General Knyphausen issued the order for what would become the last offensive campaign and pitched battles in the northern theater. "On the 6th of June we sail'd with as many troops as could safely be spared from the defense of this Province—6000—to Staten Island."[700]

The troops who began staging on the island were an impressive array, including the elite Coldstream Guards[701] and nearly a dozen battle-tested regiments of British and Hessian infantry and cavalry.[702] It was clear that

Knyphausen intended to inflict a mortal blow to the Continental army at Morristown.

The British divided their forces into three divisions. The advanced guard consisted of some of the Coldstream Guards and Skinner's Brigade, who crossed the Arthur Kill under the cover of darkness and established a beachhead. In a small skirmish in Elizabethtown at the waterfront terminus of present-day Elizabeth Avenue, the British general Thomas Stirling (not to be confused with Lord Stirling) was shot with a near-fatal wound, causing Knyphausen to take command of the advance himself.[703] Soon, the British soldiers and engineers had created a bridge of pontoon boats to connect Staten Island with another body of land for the first time in its history. This feat was described in a contemporary sketch of the battlefield and confirmed eyewitness accounts[704] and would not be replicated for over one hundred years. Knyphausen had entered Elizabethtown via Elizabeth Avenue by daybreak on June 7, and soon, the army, with its cavalry and light artillery, was on the way toward Morristown via the town of Union, then known as Connecticut Farms.[705]

There, the American militia mustered itself, fighting house to house and tree line to tree line, and put up enough resistance to halt Knyphausen's forces. At some point, the Hessian commander realized that the true strength of the American forces was more than he had anticipated and decided to retreat to some hastily thrown-up redoubts at Elizabethtown, which he ordered built to protect his bridge and resupply route.[706] Before doing so, his men committed one of the most heinous acts of the war.

After repeated harassment by snipers, the British began burning Elizabethtown and shooting the occupants of some of the houses. In one, Hannah, the wife of the Reverend Caldwell who was in charge of returning Tory property earlier that year, was struck and killed in front of her family by a trigger-happy soldier. The Whig press had a field day with the story, and it doubtlessly motivated the spirits and some of the future actions of the New Jersey militiamen.[707]

As the battle died down, the diary of Stephen Popp noted there were "heavy losses on both sides" and that on June 8, "it took 3 boats to carry the wounded to New York."[708] Knyphausen cautiously remained at Elizabethtown for nearly two weeks, knowing that Clinton's corps would be returning from Charleston any day, which would give him the reinforcements he needed.

On June 19, Clinton landed on Staten Island.[709] Simcoe barely had time to relax at Richmond before receiving urgent orders at midnight on the twenty-

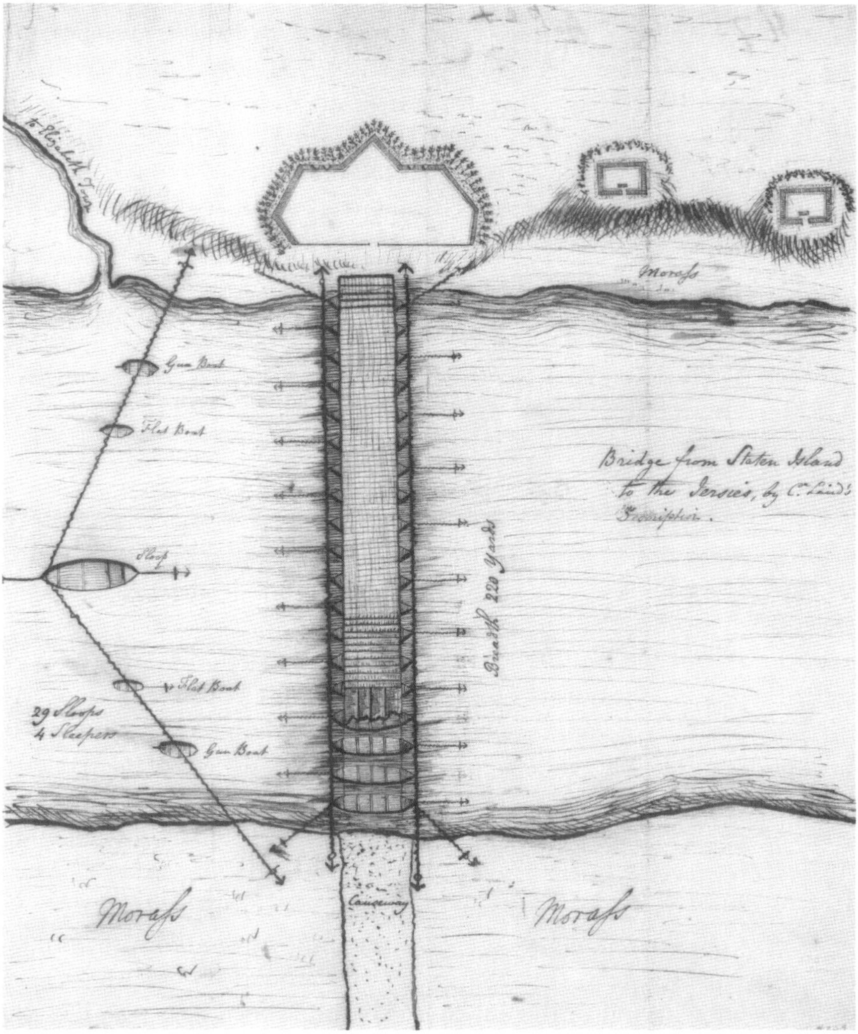

In 1780, British and Hessian forces under General Knyphausen constructed a pontoon bridge over the Arthur Kill to strike American positions at Morristown. *William L. Clements Library, University of Michigan.*

first to cross the bridge into Jersey. By nightfall the following day, the Queen's Rangers and a company of Hessian Jaeger skirmishers would each lose one man leading the vanguard of the now full-strength British brigade.[710]

They were met by General Nathanael Greene at Springfield, New Jersey. After a day of skirmishes and artillery duels, the British withdrew their entire force across the bridge as Skinner's Brigade and the Queen's

Rangers covered their retreat from the redoubts and thickets around Elizabethtown.[711] Estimates of the total killed were approximately twenty-five on each side, but the British claimed an overwhelming number of wounded, likely well over two hundred.[712] Included among the list of the dead was the rebel leader Nathaniel Fitz Randolph.[713]

For the rest of the war, no major engagements would take place in the North, although bands like the Hatfields and Fitz Randolphs would continue their work crossing the Kills. It wasn't long after his cousin's death, for example, that Asher Fitz Randolph would launch two kidnapping raids by the end of that summer.[714]

1781 AND 1782

By 1781, the war had primarily moved to the South, and major combat would conclude with the American victory at Yorktown that fall, where Simcoe would witness the capitulation.[715]

With a dwindling number of British and Hessian troops to defend the island, Richmond Town was successfully attacked by Asher Fitz Randolph in the heat of the August summer. Landing with just seventy men, he attacked the fortifications of the town, where "a severe firing commenced at daybreak and continued until 11 o'clock….All that ventured out of the fort were either killed or taken," while Fitz Randolph's own force suffered just three casualties.[716]

The rebels also became masters of the small inland waterways as the focus of the British navy shifted elsewhere in the American theater and to the larger priority of pursuing the French around the globe. In June 1781, two whaleboats and fourteen prisoners were taken from the North Shore of the island and brought to Elizabethtown. As for the British, Lieutenant Randall and his crew captured an enemy raiding party along with their gunboat in the Kills that November after an unsuccessful cattle raid near Halstead's Point,[717] the approximate location of the Goethals Bridge.[718]

In December, a small party of Jerseymen in whaleboats, likely commanded by Captain Adam Hyler, overcame three sloops in successive raids. Each sloop was armed with two three-pound cannons, two blunderbusses and a company of five sailors.[719] The next month, in retaliation, a company of Skinner's Brigade rowed quietly up the Raritan and seized all of Hyler's boats. But within a month, Skinner had built several new massive whaleboats to accommodate nearly thirty oars and was back in the fight.[720]

On a calm day in July, he put them to action against an eight-gunned tender in Raritan Bay. There was no wind that day, a nearby warship on guard was unable to intervene and the prize was dragged down into the Shrewsbury Inlet.[721] Unfortunately, a similar attempt on a galley guarding Prince's Bay a few weeks later did not end as successfully. Hyler and three boats "came up with a good deal of resolution, but Captain Cashman, who commanded the Galley, observing his motions, gave him an 18 pounder, which went through the stern of one of his boats."[722] The squadron was forced to ground their boats, where, along the South Shore coastline, they "made a smart combat" before trying to flee in the remaining two.[723] Hyler made it home that day, but it is rumored that he was poisoned at a South Amboy tavern just after this raid and died of a painful illness soon thereafter.[724]

The mantle of Captain Hyler was carried on by John Storer, who was commissioned a privateer captain by New Jersey in November 1782 and soon made a name for himself capturing an enemy vessel just beneath the battery at the Watering Place, which by then had grown to fourteen guns.[725] This may have been the last of the boat raids of the Revolution, but by that time, the war had taken a completely new form.

As noted, the British surrender at Yorktown the previous year ended major engagements, but as Staten Island's nineteenth-century chronicler J.J. Clute reminds us, "Both army organizations were maintained, though both remained passive; there was no war, there was no peace. The soldiers of both armies, having nothing else to occupy them, organized predatory expeditions in the neighborhood where they were stationed. In this respect, Staten Island was particularly unfortunate."[726] Despite the war's clear coming to an end, there was no shortage of violence, nor were there short memories of what had already occurred.

DEPREDATIONS, DISSONANCE AND DEPARTURE

Many members of the British armed forces spent their downtime in Staten Island's taverns. The Rose and Crown and the Black Horse in New Dorp were the most popular. The latter was in convenient proximity to the Egbertville Ravine, then known as the Dueling Ground, used when issues arose among patrons.[727] Many also enjoyed long afternoons at a fives' court near Port Richmond, which is a game played by hitting a ball against the walls of a three-sided enclosure.[728]

The Black Horse Tavern stood for about 150 years at the intersection of Richmond Road and Amboy Road, until its demolition in the 1930s to accommodate a street widening. *New York Public Library.*

As contemporaries recalled later on, the early part of the war passed rather smoothly, with the British typically paying for their meals in good currency and treating the inhabitants with respect. At times when they misbehaved, the soldiers were lashed and forced to make restitution.[729]

For the first two years, especially in New York Province, it was explicit British policy to not strive toward winning the hearts and minds of the population—it wasn't needed.[730] Even as late as Knyphausen's incursion into Jersey, the belief was that Loyalists were simply waiting in hiding for opportunities to come out against the rebel cause. Yet two clear British shortcomings over time actually ended up feeding a growing discontent among even their formerly most loyal subjects, including those on Staten Island. The first was a failure to restore civil government after the Howe brothers were firmly in control of the city and its immediate vicinity, and the second was the eventual breakdown of military justice as the behavior of the British and Hessian troops grew worse.[731]

This was especially true of units that were sent to Staten Island to convalesce or for winter quartering after participating in campaigns elsewhere. They simply exchanged the violence of the pitched battlefield for a front-row seat in the type of internecine warfare that occurred year-round on an island subject to raids, lawlessness and depredations. Thus Staten Island was subjected to the worst of the war far more frequently than counties elsewhere in the colonies.

Reports of robbery and abuse against women and children were normal, and rape was not unheard of. Numerous Staten Island women were subject to assaults that often resulted in pregnancies and sexually transmitted diseases.[732] In one account from a farmer near Clove Road, a son was forced to level a fatal blow against a Hessian soldier and secretly bury his body under the family home after hearing his mother scream for help.[733] Rather than crack down on these abuses, officers like Lord Rawdon chuckled about

A nineteenth-century painting depicts a British grenadier interacting with a rural woman. Encounters like this frequently occurred but were not always pleasant or welcome on Staten Island. *Brown University Library.*

"the fair nymphs of this island."[734] Court-martials were more public charade than tribunals of justice.

Sensing the pendulum swinging in the other direction, and keenly aware that there would be some retribution, Staten Island's Loyalists began to make provisions to leave even before the Treaty of Paris was signed. Prominent men like Richard Seaman and Isaac Decker, along with many of the privates who served in Skinner's Brigade and the Queen's Rangers, would find refuge and new lives in Nova Scotia. Simcoe would go on to serve as the governor of Upper Canada. Others who stuck around, like Richard Lawrence, faced the trials and confiscations that would come.[735]

For those Tories who tried to save what they could, the fight was arduous and complicated. The Confiscation Act of 1779 and the Trespass Act of 1783 essentially confiscated the property of Loyalists around the country during the war.[736] Men like Christopher Billop would start selling off property even before Yorktown, often at shillings on the pound. On May 10, 1780, he granted the first 23-acre piece of his estate to Joseph Totten, and the following May, he sold 373 acres and the manor house to Samuel Ward for £3,730. By the time the "commissioners of forfeitures" for the southern district of New York assessed Billop's remaining assets in 1784, his estate would be in the hands of nine separate owners.[737]

The loss of property and growing debt of Tories was not a priority for the new state legislatures, even in New York, which was more Loyalist than elsewhere. In 1784, the state assembly enacted "discriminatory legislation against those who had voluntarily adhered to the British during the war," including prohibitions on voting and holding office, which likely affected almost two-thirds of Richmond County.[738] From his new home in St. John, New Brunswick, Billop applied for financial relief from the British government. He estimated his estate, back pay and loss of chattel to be worth £5,171. He was granted just £400 from Parliament.[739]

But before all of the proceedings and fallout over men like Billop would occur, the most important provision of the Treaty of Paris had to be abided—the British surrender of New York City, harkening the true end of the conflict.

AFTER SEVEN YEARS OF occupation, New York was liberated of its British garrison on November 25, 1783, when Sir Guy Carleton, the last commander of His Majesty's forces, officially evacuated his troops from the fort in Manhattan. However, on Staten Island, where the occupation started

On evacuation day, November 25, 1783, the British garrison departed New York City, though it would take them over a week to stock their ships and depart from Staten Island. *Library of Congress.*

earlier than that of the city, the British would remain for nearly two weeks as provisions and passengers were gathered along its shorefront.[740]

By this point, Staten Islanders, and perhaps metaphorically the island itself, were not sorrowful of the British departure. Its forests were all but gone, its hills were formed into redoubts, its churches and other important buildings had been burned, its homes were long occupied, families were divided and countless crimes had gone unpunished.[741] So, despite the island's reputation as a Tory stronghold, it wasn't a surprise that crowds turned out on the heights of the Narrows to see the English fleet off.

From his flagship anchored just off the Watering Place, Carleton wrote his last message to Washington, informing him that his departure would take place on December 4, to which the victorious general wished him and the last British troops a "safe and pleasant passage."[742] The newspaper reported the ships under sail on the same day and in the same article that reported Washington's farewell to his generals at Fraunce's Tavern.[743]

From Staten Island, an eyewitness remembered the spectacle:

> *We stood on the heights at the Narrows, and looked down upon the decks of their ships as they passed; we were very boisterous in our demonstrations of joy; we shouted, we clapped our hands, we waved our hats, we sprang into the air, and some few, who had brought muskets with them, fired a feu-de-joie; a few others, in the exuberance of their gladness, indulged in gestures, which though very expressive, were neither polite nor judicious. The British could not look upon the scene without making some demonstration of resentment. A large seventy-four* [gunned ship], *as she was passing, fired a shot which struck the bank a few feet beneath the spot upon which were standing…It was long after dark when the last ship passed through the Narrows.*[744]

After witnessing and nearly receiving the final shot of the war, those atop Staten Island's heights were among the last Americans to lose sight of the British forces as they traveled over the horizon and far away from the new nation.

NOTES

Introduction

1. *New York Sun*, "Aquahonga," November 12, 1896.
2. George Lankevich, *New York City: A Short History* (New York: New York University Press, 2002), 6.
3. J.J. Clute, *Annals of Staten Island, From its Discovery to the Present Time* (New York: Press of Chas. Vogt, 1877), preface.
4. Ibid.

Chapter 1

5. Charles W. Leng and William T. Davis, *Staten Island and Its People: A History, 1629–1929*, vol. 1 (New York: Lewis Historical, 1930–33), 74–76.
6. Buckingham Smith, *An Inquiry into the Documents Concerning a Discovery in North America Claimed to Have Been Made by Verrazzano Read before the New York Historical Society, Tuesday, October 4th, 1864* (New York: John F. Trow, 1864), 13.
7. George W. Greene, *The Life and Voyages of Verrazzano* (Cambridge, MA: Fulsom, Wells and Thurston, 1837), 4–8.
8. Smith, *Inquiry into the Documents*, 12–13.
9. *Relatione di Giovanni da Verrazzano Fiorentino, Della Terra Per Lui Scoperta in Nome Di Sua Maestá, Scritta in Dieppa, Adi 8. Luglio. M.D.XXIIII (Navigazoni et Viaggi da Giovanni-Battista Ramusio. III. Vol. fol. Venetia. Tomo III. M.D.LVI.)*

Translated from the original Italian by Joseph G. Cogswell, Esq., member of the New York Historical Society etcetera Collections of the New York Historical Society. Second Series. Vol. I. New York. 1841. Quoted in Smith, *An Inquiry into the Documents*, 13.

10. Ibid.
11. Ibid.
12. Ibid.
13. Ibid.
14. Duncan Hunter, *Half Moon: Henry Hudson and the Voyage that Redrew the Map of the New World* (New York: Bloomsbury Press, 2009), 136–37.
15. Edwin G. Burrows and Mike Wallace, *Gotham: A History of New York City to 1898* (New York: Oxford University Press, 1999), 12.
16. Leng and Davis, *Staten Island*, vol. 1, 79.
17. Richard M. Bayles, ed., *History of Richmond County (Staten Island) New York, From Its Discovery to the Present Time* (New York: I.E. Preston & Co., 1887), 1.
18. "Staten Island Indian History," in *Annual Report of the American Scenic and Historic Preservation Society to the Legislature of the State of New York*, Vol. 22 (Albany, NY: J.B. Lyon Company, 1917), 227.
19. Robert S. Grumet, *Manhattan to Minisink: American Indian Place Names in Greater New York and Vicinity* (Norman: University of Oklahoma Press, 2013), 26. Grumet believes *Aquahonga* stems from the Munsee word for "that which is protected from the wind" but confirms the full *Aquahonga Manacknong* was used in the third and final deed delivering the title to Staten Island to the Dutch.
20. Leng and Davis, *Staten Island*, vol. 1, 72.
21. Jean R. Soderlund, *Lenape Country: Delaware Valley Society Before William Penn* (Philadelphia: University of Pennsylvania Press, 2015), 18.
22. Clute, *Annals of Staten Island*, 6.
23. Leng and Davis, *Staten Island*, vol. 1, 71.
24. Burrows and Wallace, *Gotham*, 5–6.
25. Ibid., 8.
26. Leng and Davis, *Staten Island*, vol. 1, 80.
27. Alanson Skinner, "The Lenape Indians of Staten Island," *Anthropological Papers of the Museum of Natural History, Vol III, The Indians of Greater New York and the Lower Hudson* (New York: Oder of the Trustees, 1909), 4.
28. Ibid., 5–7.
29. Ibid., 8–9.
30. *New Discoveries at Old Place: The Story of Old Place Neck, Staten Island, New York* (Pautucket, RI: Public Archaeology Laboratory, 2012), http://

www.palinc.com/sites/default/files/publications/Old_Place_Neck_Site.pdf.

31. "A Compilation of Fluted Points of Eastern North America by Count and Distribution: An AENA Project," *Archaeology of Eastern North America* 10 (Fall 1982): 27–46. Beth Wellman is the author of the section on New York.

32. Anne-Marie Cantwell and Diana de Zeriga Wall, *Unearthing Gotham: The Archaeology of New York* (New Haven, CT: Yale University Press, 2001), 39–42.

33. Skinner, "Lenape Indians," 10–17.

34. Ibid., 10.

35. "Atlas of the City of New York, Borough of Richmond. From Actual Surveys and Original Plans, by George W. and Walter S. Bromley," New York Public Library, NYPL Map Warper: Layer 1035, http://maps.nypl.org/warper/layers/1035#Show_tab (hereafter cited as NYPL Map Warper). NYPL's Map Warper is a tool that overlays historical maps of New York City over the modern street grid. In this case, a map of 1917 is used to locate the places referenced by anthropologist Alanson Skinner in 1909.

36. Skinner, "Lenape Indians," 11.

37. NYPL Map Warper: Layer 869, http://maps.nypl.org/warper/layers/869. As a point of interest, the author funded the construction of the dog run at this site and cut the ribbon just weeks before learning through his research that it had been at the heart of the Burial Ridge site.

38. Skinner, "Lenape Indians," 11–12.

39. Jerome Jacobson, "Archaeology at Tottenville Staten Island," *Bulletin: New York State Archaeological Association*, no. 23 (November 1961): 5–10.

40. Ibid.; Skinner, "Lenape Indians," 12–15.

41. Jacobson, "Archaeology at Tottenville," 7.

42. Julie A. Horn, *Phase IA Archaeological Documentary Study. New York City Department of Environmental Protection Wards Point Infrastructure Improvements Amboy Road from Wards Point Avenue to U.S. Pierhead and Bulkhead Line Staten Island, Richmond County, New York* (New York: Hazen and Sawyer, 2011), http://s-media.nyc.gov/agencies/lpc/arch_reports/1353.pdf.

43. Ed Platt to Dr. Cece Saunders, May 1, 2001, in Edward J. Lenik and Nancy L. Gibbs, *Phase IA Cultural Resources Sensitivity Evaluation: South Richmond Drainage Plans: Conference House Park Watershed, Staten Island, New York* (New York: Prepared for Historical Perspectives, Inc., 2001), Appendix B, http://s-media.nyc.gov/agencies/lpc/arch_reports/937.pdf.

44. John T. Cunningham, introduction to Robert Juet, *Juet's Journal: The Voyage of the Half Moon from 4 April to 7 November 1609*, ed. Robert M. Lunny (Newark: New Jersey Historical Society, 1959), vii–x.
45. Juet, *Juet's Journal*, 27–28.
46. Ibid., 28.
47. Ibid.
48. Ibid., 29.
49. Ibid.
50. Ibid., 29–30.
51. Ibid., 30.
52. Ibid.
53. Ibid., 35.
54. Ibid.
55. Ibid., 35–36.
56. Ira K. Morris, *Morris's Memorial History of Staten Island, New York*, vol. 1 (New York: Memorial Publishing, 1898), 24.
57. Bayles, *History of Richmond County*, 1; Ira K. Morris, "Early History of Staten Island," in *Proceedings of the New York Historical Association: The Nineteenth Annual Meeting, with Constitution, By-Laws, and List of Members* (New York: New York State Historical Association, 1919), 184.
58. Morris, *Morris's Memorial*, 24. Morris is sometimes sensational and relies on local legend.
59. Ibid., 25.
60. Burrows and Wallace, *Gotham*, 19.
61. Ibid., 18–19.
62. Morris, *Morris's Memorial*, 25.
63. Burrows and Wallace, *Gotham*, 19.
64. Ibid., 21.

Chapter 2

65. Ibid., 20–21.
66. Ibid., 20.
67. David Steven Cohen, "How Dutch Were the Dutch of New Amsterdam?" *New York History* 62, no. 1 (January 1981): 50–54, http://www.jstor.org.dbgateway.nysed.gov/stable/23169630.

68. Oliver A. Rink, "The People of New Netherland: Notes on Non-English Immigration to New York in the Seventeenth Century," *New York History* 62, no. 1 (January 1981): 4–42.
69. Eric J. Dolin, *Fur, Fortune, and Empire: The Epic History of the Fur Trade in America* (New York: W.W. Norton, 2010), 33; C.F. Hoffman, *The Pioneers of New York. An Anniversary Discourse Delivered before the St. Nicolas Society of Manhattan. Delivered December 6, 1847* (New York: Sanford and Swords, 1848), 25.
70. Clute, *Annals of Staten Island*, 15; Bayles, *History of Richmond County*, 62.
71. Mariana Griswold Van Rennselaer, *History of New York in the Seventeenth Century*, Vol. 1 (New York: Macmillan, 1909; New York: Cosimo, 2007), 69–70.
72. William Dunlap, *History of New Netherlands, Province of New York, and State of New York*, Vol. 1 (New York: Carter and Thorp, 1839; New York: Cosimo, 2008), 46–47.
73. Ariaen van der Donk, *Description of the New Netherlands*, trans. Jeremiah Johnson (Boston: Directors of the Old South Work, 1896), 9, https://archive.org/details/descriptionofnew00donc. Originally published in 1655.
74. Leng and Davis, *Staten Island*, vol. 1, 88.
75. Burrows and Wallace, *Gotham*, 21–23.
76. New Netherland Research Center, "Translation of Pieter Schaghen's 1626 Letter, Which Mentions the Purchase of Manhattes (Manhattan)," New York State Library, updated May 4, 2017, http://www.nysl.nysed.gov/newnetherland/schaghentrans.htm.
77. Burrows and Wallace, *Gotham*, 24.
78. Ibid., 29.
79. Bayles, *History of Richmond County*, 63.
80. Burrows and Wallace, *Gotham*, 22, 28.
81. Warren George Sherwood, "The Patroons of New Netherland," *Quarterly Journal of the New York State Historical Association* 12, no. 3 (July 1931): 271–94, 289–90.
82. Morris, *Morris's Memorial*, 27.
83. "Staten Island Indian History," *Annual Report of the American Scenic and Historic Preservation Society*, 229.
84. Burrows and Wallace, *Gotham*, 28.
85. Murray D. Rothbard, *Conceived in Liberty* (New York: Arlington House Publishers, 1979; Auburn, AL: Ludvig von Mises Institute, 1999), 291.
86. Burrows and Wallace, *Gotham*, 29.

87. David Pietersz de Vries, "Korte Historiael Ende Journaels Aenteyckeninge," in *Narratives of New Netherland 1609–1664*, ed. J. Franklin Jameson (New York: Charles Scribner and Sons, 1909), 199.
88. Ibid., 202.
89. Bayles, *History of Richmond County*, 64.
90. Burrows and Wallace, *Gotham*, 30.
91. Clute, *Annals of Staten Island*, 18.
92. De Vries, "Korte Historiael Ende," 211.
93. Ibid.; Clute, *Annals of Staten Island*, 19–20. The translation of de Vries's original text does not make it clear whether it was Kieft or Melyn who sought permission to distill on Staten Island. However, popular history seems to credit Kieft as the first distiller in the United States.
94. Morris, *Morris's Memorial*, 34.
95. Burrows and Wallace, *Gotham*, 37–38.
96. Morris, *Morris's Memorial*, 34.
97. The Anglicized Algonquian word for "chief."
98. Burrows and Wallace, *Gotham*, 38.
99. De Vries, "Korte Historiael Ende," 211.
100. Morris, *Morris's Memorial*, 136; Mark Meuwese, *Brothers in Arms, Partners in Trade: Dutch-Indigenous Alliances in the Atlantic World, 1595–1674* (Leiden, NL: Brill, 2012), 245. The quote is from Morris; however, the idea of a wampum ransom comes from many other sources, including Meuwese.
101. De Vries, "Korte Historiael Ende," 211.
102. Meuwese, *Brothers in Arms*, 245.
103. Burrows and Wallace, *Gotham*, 38.
104. De Vries, "Korte Historiael Ende," 228.
105. Burrows and Wallace, *Gotham*, 39.
106. Ibid.
107. Willem Frijhoff, *Fulfilling God's Mission: The Two Worlds of Dominie Everardus Bogardus, 1607–1647* (Leiden, NL: Brill, 2007), 491.
108. "Staten Island Indian History," *Annual Report of the American Scenic and Historic Preservation Society*, 232.
109. Burrows and Wallace, *Gotham*, 39.
110. Ibid., 42.
111. Ibid., 48–50.
112. Ibid., 62.
113. Leng and Davis, *Staten Island*, vol. 1, 99.
114. Sherwood, "Patroons of New Netherland," 290.
115. Melyn, as quoted in Leng and Davis, *Staten Island*, vol. 1, 99.

116. Cornelius Melyn to the West India Company, 1659, Melyn Papers, 1640–99, in *Collections of the New York Historical Society for the Year 1913* (New York: New York Historical Society, 1914), 113.
117. Leng and Davis, *Staten Island*, vol. 1, 101.
118. Melyn to the West India Company, 113.
119. Lankevich, *New York City*, 6.
120. Sherwood, "Patroons of New Netherland," 290.
121. Bayles, *History of Richmond County*, 68.
122. Ibid.
123. Leng and Davis, *Staten Island*, vol. 1, 100.
124. Cornelius Melyn to the West India Company, 1659, 113.
125. Burrows and Wallace, *Gotham*, 68.
126. Ibid.; Jaap Jacobs, "'Hot Pestilential and Unheard-of Fevers, Illnesses, and Torments': Days of Fasting and Prayer in New Netherland," *New York History* 96, no. 3–4 (Summer/Fall 2015): 284–300, 284.
127. Leng and Davis, *Staten Island*, vol. 1, 101.
128. Cornelius Melyn to the West India Company, 1659, 114.
129. Ibid.
130. Ibid., 115.
131. Ibid.
132. Leng and Davis, *Staten Island*, vol. 1, 102.
133. Ibid.
134. "Staten Island Indian History," *Annual Report of the American Scenic and Historic Preservation Society*, 232.
135. Bayles, *History of Richmond County*, 70.
136. Leng and Davis, *Staten Island*, vol. 1, 103.
137. Bayles, *History of Richmond County*, 70.
138. Leng and Davis, *Staten Island*, vol. 4, 354.
139. Anne-Claire Faucquez, "Les Réfugiés Huguenots au Coeur de la Mosaique Ethno-Religieuse de la Colonie de New York: Une Assimilation Partielle ou Complète? (1670–1730)," *Bulletin de la Société de l'Histoire de Protestantisme Français (1903–)* 155 (Octobre–Novembre–Décembre 2009): 795–808.
140. Ralph LeFevre, "The Huguenots—The First Settlers in the Province of New York," *Quarterly Journal of the New York State Historical Association* 19 (1921): 177–85.
141. Owen Stanwood, "Between Eden and Empire: Huguenot Refugees and the Promise of New Worlds," *American Historical Review* 118, no. 5 (December 2013): xvi, 1, 319–44.

142. Susanne Lachenicht, "Huguenot Immigrants and the Formation of National Identities, 1548–1787," *Historical Journal* 50, no. 2 (June 2007): 309–31.
143. Faucquez, "Les Réfugiés Huguenots," 795–96.
144. David William Vorhees, "Huguenots," in *Encyclopedia of New York*, 2nd edition, ed. Kenneth T. Jackson (New Haven, CT: Yale University Press, 2010), 628–29.
145. "Extract from a Letter of Stuyvesant to the Directors: Fortifications on Long and Staten Island; John Scott, and the English on Long Island. (April 26, 1664)," in *Documents Relating to the Colonial History of the State of New York*, ed. B. Fernow, vol. 14, *Documents Relating to the History of the Early Colonial Settlements Principally on Long Island, with a Map of Its Western Part, Made in 1666* (Albany, NY: Weed, Parsons and Company, 1883), 546.
146. Stephen Weinstein, "New Utrecht," *Encyclopedia of New York*, 2nd edition, ed. Kenneth T. Jackson (New Haven, CT: Yale University Press, 2010), 907.
147. "Extract from a Letter of Stuyvesant to the Directors," *Documents Relating to the Colonial History*.
148. Ibid.
149. John T. McNeill, *The History and Character of Calvinism* (New York: Oxford University Press, 1954), 279.
150. Leng and Davis, *Staten Island*, vol. 1, 104.
151. "Extract from a Letter of Stuyvesant to the Directors," *Documents Relating to the Colonial History*.
152. Leng and Davis, *Staten Island*, vol. 1, 104.
153. NYPL Map Warper: Layer 1035.
154. Leng and Davis, *Staten Island*, vol. 1, 104.
155. Historic Richmondtown, "Billiou-Stillwell-Perine Site," historicrichmondtown.org.
156. Leng and Davis, *Staten Island*, vol. 1, 104.
157. Lucian J. Fosdick, *The French Blood in America* (New York: Baker and Taylor, 1911), 217.
158. Phyllis DeLisio and Rose Stella Proscia, "SI350 and the Memorial Church of the Huguenots," http://huguenotparkchurch.org/wp-content/uploads/2012/03/History_of_the_French_Huguenots-history_book-updated-20121.pdf.
159. Historic Richmondtown, "Voorlezer's House," historicrichmondtown.org.
160. Historic Richmondtown, "New Details Come to Light About the Voorlezer's House at Historic Richmond Town," historicrichmondtown.org.

161. Andrew Dolkhart and New York City Landmarks Preservation Commission, *Guide to New York City Landmarks* (New York: John Wiley and Sons, 2008), 388.
162. George Tuttle, "The Town of Dover," *Quarterly Journal of the New York State Historical Association* 19 (1921): 164–76.
163. Jaspar Danckaerts, entry of Wednesday, October 11, 1679, *The Journal of Jaspar Danckaerts, 1769–1680*, eds. Bartlett Burleigh James and J. Franklin Jameson (New York: Charles Scribner's Sons, 1913; Project Gutenberg Ebook #23258, 2007), 71–72.
164. Leng and Davis, *Staten Island*, vol. 1, 105.
165. Ibid., 430.
166. Rev. Henry Selyns to the Classis of Amsterdam, September 14, 1690, quoted in Leng and Davis, *Staten Island*, vol. 1, 432–33.
167. Leng and Davis, *Staten Island*, vol. 1, 433.
168. John Miller, *New York Considered and Improved, 1695*, ed. Victor Hugo Paltsits (Cleveland, OH: Burrows Company, 1903), appendix 4, 117.
169. Ibid., 54.
170. Kenneth M. Gold and Lori Weintrob, *Discovering Staten Island: A 350th Anniversary Commemorative History* (Charleston, SC: The History Press, 2011), 192–93.
171. Leng and Davis, *Staten Island*, vol. 1, 104.
172. Ibid., 105.
173. "Extract from a Letter of Stuyvesant to the Directors," *Documents Relating to the Colonial History*.
174. Dallas Irvine, "The First British Regulars in North America," *Military Affairs* 9, no. 4 (Winter 1945): 337–54.
175. Ibid., 344.
176. Ibid. After the disbandment of the New Model Army at the conclusion of the English Civil War, Charles II formed the first standing regiments of English, Irish and Scottish troops. Nicolls had command of a company.

Chapter 3

177. Irvine, "First British Regulars," 337.
178. Gijs Rommelse, "The Role of Mercantilism in Anglo-Dutch Political Relations, 1650–74," *Economic History Review* 63, no. 3 (August 2010): 591–611.

179. Martha Joanna Lamb, *History of the City of New York: Its Origin, Rise, and Progress* (New York: A.S. Barnes, 1877), 192–96.
180. Bayles, *History of Richmond County*, 72.
181. Lamb, *History of the City*, 199.
182. John S.C. Abbott, *Peter Stuyvesant, the Last Dutch Governor of New Amsterdam* (New York: Dodd & Mead, 1873), 259, 291.
183. "Extract from a Letter of Stuyvesant to the Directors," *Documents Relating to the Colonial History*, 548.
184. Abbott, *Peter Stuyvesant*, 289–90.
185. Irvine, "First British Regulars," 337.
186. Burrows and Wallace, *Gotham*, 73.
187. Lamb, *History of the City*, 214.
188. Joyce D. Goodfriend, *Before the Melting Pot: Society and Culture in Colonial New York City, 1664–1730* (Princeton, NJ: Princeton University Press, 1992), 64.
189. Burrows and Wallace, *Gotham*, 77.
190. Ibid., 78.
191. Leng and Davis, *Staten Island*, vol. 1, 415.
192. Ibid., 118.
193. "A Warrant from the Governor to the Inhabitants of Staten Island, Empowering Them to Chuse Civill Officers (7 September 1667)," in *Documents Relating to the Colonial History of the State of New York*, ed. B. Pernow, vol. 13, *Documents Relating to the History and Settlements of the Towns along the Hudson and Mohawk Rivers, from 1630 to 1684* (Albany, NY: Weed, Parsons and Company, 1881), 415–16.
194. Leng and Davis, *Staten Island*, vol. 1, 113.
195. Ibid.
196. Historic Richmondtown, "Billiou-Stillwell-Perine Site," historicrichmondtown.org.
197. Burrows and Wallace, *Gotham*, 73.
198. Historical Notes, in *The Colonial Laws of New York from the Year 1664 to the Revolution*, vol. 1 (Albany, NY: J.B. Lyon, State Printer, 1894), xi–xii.
199. Ibid., "Nicolls' Proclaimation Revoking the Dutch and Establishing the English Form of Government, 1665. (12 June 1665)," 100–1.
200. Ibid.; Historical Notes, *Colonial Laws of New York*, vol. 1, xii; Leng and Davis, *Staten Island*, vol. 1, 125.
201. Ibid., "Orders Made at the Generall Court of Assizes Held in New Yorke, Beginning on the 6th and Ending on the 13th Day of October in the 27th Yeare of His Majesties Reigne Anno Domini 1675," 100.

202. Leng and Davis, *Staten Island*, vol. 1, 125. Thankfully, the records have been transcribed into John E. Stillwell *Historical and Genealogical Miscellany: Data Relating to the Settlement and Settlers of New York and New Jersey*, ed. John Stillwell, vol. 1 (New York: New York State, 1903).
203. Court record of October 3, 1680; Stillwell, *Historical and Genealogical Miscellany*, 2.
204. Stillwell, *Historical and Genealogical Miscellany*, 2; Court record of June 6, 1681, 4.
205. Stillwell, *Historical and Genealogical Miscellany*, 2; Court record of June 6, 1681, 4; Testimony of Richard Taterfall, January 15, 1681, 11; Testimony of Elizabeth Lawrence, January 16, 1681, 11; Court record of April 21, 1681, 19.
206. Lamb, *History of the City*, 302.
207. Leng and Davis, *Staten Island*, vol. 1, 133.
208. Lamb, *History of the City*, 303.
209. "An Act to Divide the Province and Dependencies into Shires and Counties, Passed November 1st 1683," in *Documents Relating to the Colonial History of the State of New York*, vol. 13, 575.
210. Bayles, *History of Richmond County*, 90.
211. "An Act for the Further Laying Out, Regulating and Better Clearing Publick High-Ways throughout This Colony [Passed October 23, 1713]," in *Colonial Laws of New York*, vol. 1, 799–800.
212. Leng and Davis, *Staten Island*, vol. 1, 159–61.
213. "List of Towns," *The Revised Statutes of the State of New York, as Altered by the Legislature; Including the Statutory Provisions of a General Nature, Passed from 1828 to 1835 Inclusive; With References to Judicial Decisions; to Which Are Added, Certain Local Acts Passed Before and Since the Revised Statutes; All the Acts of General Interest Passed During the Session of 1836; and an Appendix, Containing Extracts from the Original Reports of the Revisers to the Legislature, All Material Notes Which Accompanied Those Reports, and Explanatory Remarks*, vol. 3 (Albany, NY: Packard and Van Benthuysen, 1836), 308.
214. Leng and Davis, *Staten Island*, vol. 1, 113.
215. Ibid.
216. "Staten Island Indian History," *Annual Report of the American Scenic and Historic Preservation Society*, 233–39.
217. "Indian Deed of Staten Island, 1670," in *Minutes of the Executive Council of the Province of New York: Administration of Francis Lovelace 1668–1673*, ed. Victor H. Paltsits, vol. 1, *Minutes; Collateral and Illustrative Documents I–XIX* (Albany, NY: J.B. Lyon Company, State Printers, 1910), 342.

218. Ibid.
219. Andrew Lipman, "Buying and Selling Staten Island: The Curious Case of the 1670 Deed to Aquehonga Manacknong," *Common-Place* 15, no. 2 (Winter 2015), http://www.common-place-archives.org.
220. "Letter from Gov Lovelace to the Governor of Bermuda Concerning Immigration (3 June 1669)," in *Documents Relating to the Colonial History of the State of New York*, Vol. 13, 424–25.
221. "Propositions and Condicons for a Competent Number of Familyes from Ye Island Barmudas to Settle a Township upon Staten-Island, Belonging to These His Royal Highnesse Territoryes," in *Documents Relating to the Colonial History of the State of New York*, vol. 13, 425.
222. "Mr. Jacques Cortilleau Ordered and Appointed for Ye Convenient Laying out 40 Lotts for Ye Settling of 2 Townships on Staten-Island (24 October 1670)," in *Documents Relating to the Colonial History of the State of New York*, vol. 13, 458.
223. Van Rennselaer, *History of New York*, 416–17.
224. "A Proclamation About Ye Lotts Granted on Staten-Island, Enjoining Those Persons Who Have Promises of Land There, to Bring in Their Names to the Secretaries Office, and Within a Certain Time to Fence in Ye Same," in *Minutes of the Executive Council of the Province of New York. Administration of Francis Lovelace. 1668–1673*, vol. 2 (Albany: State of New York, 1910), 490.
225. Leng and Davis, *Staten Island*, vol. 1, 117.
226. New York City Landmarks Preservation Commission, "Lakeman House. Research Staff Hearing Statement (2010)," Backlog Initiative: Addressing 95 Properties, http://www.nyc.gov.
227. "Council Minute. Encouragement of Immigration: Staten Island Land Matters," in *Documents Relating to the Colonial History of the State of New York*, vol. 13, 485.
228. Leng and Davis, *Staten Island*, vol. 1, 120.
229. NYPL Map Warper: Layer 869.
230. Leng and Davis, *Staten Island*, vol. 1, 120.
231. Clute, *Annals of Staten Island*, 210.
232. Jaspar Danckaerts, entries of Wednesday October 11, 1679 to Friday October 13, 1679, *Journal of Jaspar Danckaerts*, 69–75.
233. Charles F. Billopp, *A History of Thomas and Anne Billopp Farmar, and Some of Their Descendants in America* (New York: Grafton Press, 1907), 17–18.
234. William T. Davis, *The Conference or Billopp House* (Staten Island, NY: Staten Island Historical Society, 1926), 7.

235. Artyom Anikin, "The Lost Soldier of Orange: A Brief Biography of Governor Anthony Colve, 1644–1693," *New York History* 96, no. 3–4 (Summer/Fall 2015): 336–53.
236. Davis, *Conference of Billopp House*, 7.
237. "Council Minute," *Documents Relating to the Colonial History*, 485.
238. Davis, *Conference of Billopp House*, 50–51.
239. Bayles, *History of Richmond County*, 108.
240. Leng and Davis, *Staten Island*, vol. 1, 129.
241. Davis, *Conference of Billopp House*, 51.
242. "The Duke of York's Release to John Lord Berkeley, and Sir George Carteret, 24th of June, 1664," in *The Federal and State Constitutions, Colonial Charters, and Other Organic Laws of the State, Territories, and Colonies Now Heretofore Forming the United States of America*, ed. Francis Newton Thorpe, vol. 5 (Washington, D.C.: U.S. Government Printing Office, 1909), 2,534.
243. Billopp, *History of Thomas and Anne*, 18.
244. Leng and Davis, *Staten Island*, vol. 1, 132.
245. Ibid., 129.
246. John Charnock, *Biographia Navalis; or, Impartial Memoirs of the Lives and Characters of the Officers of the Navy of Great Britain from the Year 1660 to the Present Time*, vol. 1 (London: R. Faulder, 1794), 386–87.
247. Leng and Davis, *Staten Island*, vol. 1, 129.
248. Bayles, *History of Richmond County*, 106.
249. Lamb, *History of the City*, 300.
250. Bayles, *History of Richmond County*, 119.
251. Edward Channing, "Colonel Thomas Dongan, Governor of New York," in *Proceedings of the American Antiquarian Society* 18 (October 1906–October 1907): 336–37.
252. Ibid., 339–45.
253. Lamb, *History of the City*, 303.
254. Leng and Davis, *Staten Island*, vol. 1, 128.
255. "An Act for Rewarding of Those Who Destroy Wolves [Passed November 1, 1683]," in *Colonial Laws of New York*, vol. 1, 133.
256. Leng and Davis, *Staten Island*, vol. 1, 133.
257. Ibid.
258. "An Act for the Raising and Levying of Two Thousand Pounds for Paying and Defraying the Incidentall Charges, According to Establishment of One Hundred Fusileers with Their Officers for One Whole Yeare [Passed, May 13, 1691]," in *Colonial Laws of New York*, vol. 1, 240.

259. "An Act for the raising and paying One hundred and fifty men to be forthwith raised for the Defence and reinforcement of Albany for six months. [Passed September 29, 1691]," in *Colonial Laws of New York*, vol. 1, 258–59.
260. "An Act for the Raising of Two Hundred Men with Their Proper Officers for the Securing and Reinforcing of Albany in the Frontiers of This Province. [Passed, April 29, 1692]," in *Colonial Laws of New York*, vol. 1, 274.
261. Bayles, *History of Richmond County*, 120–21.
262. "Les Dragonnades (1681–1685)," Musée Virtuel du Protestantisme, https://www.museeprotestant.org/.
263. Leng and Davis, *Staten Island*, vol. 1, 134.
264. Ibid.
265. Robert J. Brugger, *Maryland, A Middle Temperament: 1634–1980* (Baltimore, MD: Johns Hopkins University Press, 1988), 49.
266. Lamb, *History of the City*, 350.
267. Berthold Fernow, ed., *New York Council Calendar of Council Minutes, 1668–1783* (Albany: University of the State of New York, 1902), 64.
268. Leng and Davis, *Staten Island*, vol. 1, 135.
269. Bayles, *History of Richmond County*, 97.
270. Ibid., 96.
271. "Commission of Cornelis Corsen as Infantry Captain for Northeast Richmond County," in *The Leisler Papers, 1689–1691: Files of the Provincial Secretary of New York Relating to the Administration of Lieutenant-Governor Jacob Leisler*, ed. Peter R. Cristoph (Syracuse, NY: Syracuse University Press, 2002), 336; "Commission of Cornelis Nevius as Ensign in Corsen's Company," in *Leisler Papers*, 336.
272. "List of Soldiers for the Expedition Against Canada," in *Leisler Papers*, 133.
273. Bayles, *History of Richmond County*, 100.
274. "An Act for the Regulating the Damages Done in the Time of the Late Disorders and for the Uniting of the Minds of Their Majestyes Subjects That Have Lately Absented Themselves from Their Habitations and the Usuall Places of Their Abode. [Passed, September 30, 1691]," in *Colonial Laws of New York*, vol. 1, 262.
275. Tobias Alexander Wright, ed, "Dutch Reformed Church Records of Port Richmond," in *Collections of the New York Geneological and Biographical Society*, vol. 4, *Staten Island Church Records* (New York: Printed for the Society, 1908), 33.

276. Edward T. Corwin, *A Manual of the Reformed Church in America (formerly Ref. Prot. Dutch Church) 1628–1902* (New York: Board of Publication of the Reformed Church in America, 1902), 1,012.
277. Leng and Davis, *Staten Island*, vol. 1, 436.
278. Ibid., 435.
279. Bayles, *History of Richmond County*, 352.
280. Corwin, *Manual of the Reformed Church*, 851, 852, 1,012.
281. "An Act for Settling a Ministry & Raising a Maintenance for Them in the City of New York County of Richmond Westchester and Queens County [Passed, September 22, 1693]," in *Colonial Laws of New York*, vol. 1, 328–29.
282. William T. Davis, Charles W. Leng and Royden Woodward Vosburgh, *The Church of St. Andrew, Richmond, Staten Island: Its History, Vital Records and Gravestone Inscription* (Staten Island, NY: Staten Island Historical Society, 1925), 17–18.
283. Charles T. Bridgeman and Clifford P. Morehouse, *A History of the Parish of Trinity Church in the City of New York: To the Close of the Rectorship of Dr. Inglis, A.D. 1783* (New York: Putnam, 1898), 97.
284. Davis, *Conference of Billopp House*, 18–19.
285. Leng and Davis, *Staten Island*, vol. 1, 449.
286. Davis, *Conference of Billopp House*, 22.
287. "Aeneas Mackenzie to the Secretary," July 28, 1710, as quoted in Davis, *Conference of Billopp House*, 51.
288. Davis, *Conference of Billopp House*, 27
289. "Charter of the Church of St. Andrew," as recorded in Davis, *Conference of Billopp House*, 60.
290. Leng and Davis, *Staten Island*, vol. 1, 449.
291. Ibid., 450.
292. *New York Council Calendar of Council Minutes, 1668–1783*, 157, 158, 159, 168, 178.
293. Census of Staten Island in the Year 1706, in Stillwell, *Historical and Genealogical Miscellany*, 150–56.
294. Davis, *Conference of Billopp House*, 19.
295. Liber A. Richmond Co. (N.Y.) Records, in Stillwell, *Historical and Genealogical Miscellany*, 1–56. For example, there is no listing for a "Van Dick" or similarly spelled family name in the 1706 census, but by 1728, a new earmark is recorded for Jacob Van Dick, which was then passed down to his son Zacheus Van Dyck in 1761.
296. Davis, *Conference of Billopp House*, 19.

297. Leng and Davis, *Staten Island*, vol. 1, 137.
298. "These Following Instruments Was Recorded for the Comissioners of Ye High Wayes October the 27th 1708," in Stillwell, *Historical and Genealogical Miscellany*, 52.
299. "A Road from the Head of the Fresh Kill to Captain Christopher Billopps," in Stillwell, *Historical and Genealogical Miscellany*, 53.
300. "Numerous Notes Delineating Roads," in Stillwell, *Historical and Genealogical Miscellany*, 52–55.
301. Leng and Davis, *Staten Island*, vol. 1, 148.
302. Ibid., 147, 148, 153.
303. Ibid., 501–2.
304. Mr. Mackenzie to the Secretary, May 4, 1711, as quoted in Davis, *Conference of Billopp House*, 52–53.
305. Clute, *Annals of Staten Island*, 145, 146; Morris, *Morris's Memorial*, 49.
306. NYPL Map Warper: Layer 869.
307. "The Duke of York's Laws, 1665–1675," in *Colonial Laws of New York*, vol. 1, 73.
308. Morris, *Morris's Memorial*, 49.
309. "A Bill for the Better Laying out Regulating Clearing and Preserving Publick, Comon Highways in This Colony and for the Erecting and Building of a County Jaile and County House in the County of Richmond. [Passed, June 27, 1704]," in *Colonial Laws of New York*, vol. 1, 573–74.
310. "An Act for Repealing an Exception Provisoe Mentioned & Expressed in One of General Assembly Entituled an Act for Better Laying Out Regulating Clearing & Preserving Publick Comon Highways in Colony and for the Erecting & Building County Goale & County House in the of Richmond, [Passed, June 24, 1719]," in *Colonial Laws of New York*, vol. 1, 1,024.
311. "An Act to Enable the Justices of the Peace in the County of Richmond to Build a County House and a New Goal in the Said County, [Passed, September 20, 1728]."
312. Leng and Davis, *Staten Island*, vol. 1, 147.
313. Phillip Papas, *That Ever Loyal Island* (New York: New York University Press, 2009), 13–14.
314. Leng and Davis, *Staten Island*, vol. 1, 146.
315. NYPL Map Warper: Layer 869.
316. NYPL Map Warper: Layer 1035.
317. Bayles, *History of Richmond County*, 151.
318. Ibid., 152.

319. Court of Sessions notes, as quoted in Bayles, *History of Richmond County*, 134.
320. Ibid., 14–15.
321. Leng and Davis, *Staten Island*, vol. 1, 148.
322. Bayles, *History of Richmond County*, 153.
323. Leng and Davis, *Staten Island*, vol. 1, 145.
324. Ibid.
325. "An Act for the Security & Defence of This Colony during the Expedition to Canada. [Passed, August 4, 1711]," in *Colonial Laws of New York*, vol. 1, 741.
326. Leng and Davis, *Staten Island*, vol. 1, 147, 153.

Chapter 4

327. Peter E. Russell, "Redcoats in the Wilderness: British Officers and Irregular Warfare in Europe and America, 1740 to 1760," *William and Mary Quarterly* 35, no. 4 (October 1978): 629–52.
328. F.W. Anderson, "Why Did Colonial New Englanders Make Bad Soldiers? Contractual Principles and Military Conduct during the Seven Years' War," *William and Mary Quarterly* 38, no. 3 (July 1981): 395–417.
329. Edward F. De Lancey, ed., *Muster Rolls of New York Provincial Troops, 1755–1764* (New York: Printed for the Society, 1891; Westminster, MD: Heritage Books, 2007), 54–56.
330. William Smith, *The History of the Late Province of New-York, from Its Discovery, to the Appointment of Governor Colden, in 1762*, vol. 2 (New York: New York Historical Society, 1829), 264.
331. *New-York Mercury*, "Boston, July 17. The Advices from Albany and Lake George, from June 20, to July 7," July 24, 1758.
332. *New-York Mercury*, "New-York, July 24. Extract of a Letter from a Gentleman at Lake George, Dated July 11, 1758," July 24, 1758.
333. New York State Historical Association, "Provincial Regiments at Ticonderoga," in *Proceedings of the New York State Historical Association*, vol. 10 (Glens Falls: New York Historical Association, 1911), 415–16.
334. Bayles, *History of Richmond County*, 140.
335. *New York Gazette*, "Extract of a Letter from Albany, Dated September, 17, 1758," October 2, 1758.
336. New York State Historian, *New York Colonial Muster Rolls, 1664–1775: Report of the State Historian of the State of New York*, vol. 2 (Baltimore: Genealogical Publishing, 2000), 519.

337. Jeffery Amherst, *The Journal of Jeffery Amherst, Recording the Military Career of General Amherst in America from 1758 to 1763,* ed. John C. Webster (Chicago: University of Chicago Press, 1931), 269.
338. New York State Historical Association, "Table of Losses of Black Watch in Seven Years' War," in *Proceedings of the New York State Historical Association*, 410.
339. Amherst, *Journal of Jeffery Amherst*, 269, 275, 283–86, 306.
340. *New-York Gazette*, "New-York, November 16," November 16, 1761.
341. Clute, *Annals of Staten Island*, 70.
342. Leng and Davis, *Staten Island*, vol. 1, 156.
343. Amherst, *Journal of Jeffery Amherst*, 274.
344. Bob Ruppert, "The Battle of Golden Hill—Six Weeks before the Boston Massacre," *Journal of the American Revolution* (2014), https://allthingsliberty.com.
345. Roger J. Champagne, "New York's Radicals and the Coming of Independence," *Journal of American History* 51, no. 1 (June 1964): 21–40.
346. Extract of the town records of Westfield, April 5, 1768, as quoted in Leng and Davis, *Staten Island*, vol. 1.
347. Joseph Tiedemann, "A Revolution Foiled: Queens County, New York, 1775–1776," *Journal of American History* 75, no. 2 (September 1988): 417–44.
348. David L. Holmes, "The Episcopal Church and the American Revolution," *Historical Magazine of the Protestant Episcopal Church* 47, no. 3 (September 1978): 261–91.
349. Papas, *That Ever Loyal Island*, 25.
350. Ibid.
351. Holmes, "Episcopal Church," 275.
352. Papas, *That Ever Loyal Island*, 23.
353. Ibid., 24.
354. Aaron S. Fogleman, "Moravian Immigration and Settlement in British North America, 1734–1775," *Transactions of the Moravian Historical Society* 29 (1996): 23–58.
355. John R. Weinlick, "Colonial Moravians, Their Status Among the Churches," *Pennsylvania History: A Journal of Mid-Atlantic Studies* 26, no. 3 (July 1959): 213–25.
356. John R. Weinlick, "The Moravians and the American Revolution: An Overview," *Transactions of the Moravian Historical Society* 23, no. 1 (1977): 1–16.
357. Leng and Davis, *Staten Island*, vol. 1, 157, 161–62.
358. Papas, *That Ever Loyal Island*, 26.

359. Bayles, *History of Richmond County*, 328, 330.
360. Lamb, *History of the City*, 685; Leng and Davis, *Staten Island*, vol. 1, 162.
361. Papas, *That Ever Loyal Island*, 27–28.
362. Edward Countryman, "Consolidating Power in Revolutionary America: The Case of New York, 1775–1783," *Journal of Interdisciplinary History* 6, no. 4 (Spring 1976): 645–77. Countryman uses categories developed in chapter 8 of Ted Gurr, *Why Men Rebel* (Princeton, NJ: Princeton University Press, 1974) to place each county in a matrix.
363. Bernard Mason, *The Road to Independence* (Lexington: University of Kentucky Press, 1966), 118.
364. Ibid., 29.
365. Bayles, *History of Richmond County*, 159.
366. New York (State) General Assembly, *Journal of the Votes and Proceedings of the General Assembly of the Colony of New York: From 1766 to 1776, Inclusive* (Albany, NY: Printed by J. Buel, 1820).
367. Mason, *Road to Independence*, 81.
368. Alexander C. Flick, *Loyalism in New York during the American Revolution* (New York: Columbia University Press, 1901), 48.
369. Mason, *Road to Independence*, 86.
370. Bayles, *History of Richmond County*, 159–60.
371. New York State Legislature, *Journals of the Provincial Congress, Provincial Convention, Committee of Safety and Council of Safety of the State of New-York. 1775–1775–1777*, vol. 1 (Albany, NY: T. Weed, 1842), 8.
372. Ibid.
373. Papas, *That Ever Loyal Island*, 33.
374. Flick, *Loyalism in New York*, 46.
375. Ibid., 34.
376. Flick, *Loyalism in New York*, 48–49.
377. Leng and Davis, *Staten Island*, vol. 1, 166.
378. Provincial Congress to Richmond committee, December 15, 1775, as quoted in Bayles, *History of Richmond County*, 161.
379. Leng and Davis, *Staten Island*, vol. 1, 166.
380. New York State Legislature, *Journals of the Provincial Congress, Provincial Convention, Committee of Safety and Council of Safety of the State of New-York. 1775–1775–1777*, vol. 2 (Albany, NY: T. Weed, printer to the state, 1842), 227.
381. Congress to the Committee of Safety on Recess of the Provincial Congress of New York, February 8, 1776, as quoted in Bayles, *History of Richmond County*, 163.

382. New York State Legislature, *Journals of the Provincial Congress*, vol. 1, 247.
383. Ibid.
384. New York State Legislature, *Journals of the Provincial Congress*, vol. 1, 263.
385. Leng and Davis, *Staten Island*, vol. 3, 119.
386. New York State Legislature, *Journals of the Provincial Congress*, vol. 2, 127.
387. New Jersey Legislature, *Official Register of the Officers and Men of New Jersey in the Revolutionary War* (Trenton, NJ: Wm. T. Nicholson & Co., 1872), 15.
388. New York State Legislature, *Journals of the Provincial Congress*, vol. 2, 127.
389. Ibid., vol. 1, 310.
390. New Jersey Legislature, *Minutes of the Provincial Congress and the Council of Safety of the State of New Jersey [1775–1776]* (Trenton, NJ: Naar, Day & Nar, 1879), 361–62.
391. New York State Legislature, *Journals of the Provincial Congress*, vol. 1, 310.
392. Papas, *That Ever Loyal Island*, 46–47.
393. New York State Legislature, *Journals of the Provincial Congress*, vol. 1, 315.
394. Papas, *That Ever Loyal Island*, 47.
395. Ibid., 28–29.
396. Ibid., 29.
397. New Jersey Legislature, *Minutes of the Provincial Congress*, 50–51.
398. Ibid., 54–55.
399. *Rivington's New York Gazetteer*, "Some Particulars of a Riot That Happened at Elizabeth-Town in East Jersey, on Wednesday the 8th of February," March 2, 1775.
400. Ibid.; Papas, *That Ever Loyal Island*, 30.
401. Papas, *That Ever Loyal Island*, 30; *Rivington's New York Gazetteer*, "The Substance of the Affidavit of James Johnson, of the County of Richmond, in the Province of New-York, Seaman, as Taken the 13th Day of March, 1775, before David Alson, Esq; One of His Majesty's Justices of the Peace, for the County of Middlesex, in New-Jersey, Is as Follows," March 23, 1775.
402. Vice Admiral Samuel Graves to Philip Stephens, March 4, 1775, in *Naval Documents of the American Revolution*, ed. William Bell Clark, vol. 1 (Washington, D.C.: Government Printing Office, 1964), 123–24.
403. Captain James Montagu R.N. to Vice Admiral Samuel Graves, April 26, 1775, in *Naval Documents of the American Revolution*, vol. 5, 228.
404. Vice Admiral Samuel Graves to Philip Stephens, June 16, 1775, in *Naval Documents of the American Revolution*, vol. 5, 690–91.
405. Papas, *That Ever Loyal Island*, 37.
406. Ibid., 59–60.

407. New York State Legislature, *Journals of the Provincial Congress*, vol. 1, 431.
408. Ibid., 432.
409. Leng and Davis, *Staten Island*, vol. 4, 456.
410. New York State Legislature, *Journals of the Provincial Congress*, vol. 1, 432.
411. Papas, *That Ever Loyal Island*, 40–41.
412. Joseph S. Tiedemann, *Reluctant Revolutionaries: New York City and the Road to Independence, 1763–1776* (Ithaca, NY: Cornell University Press, 1997), 241.
413. Papas, *That Ever Loyal Island*, 45, 48.
414. Tiedemann, "Revolution Foiled," 429–30.
415. Tiedemann, *Reluctant Revolutionaries*, 242.
416. Barnet Schecter, *The Battle for New York: The City at the Heart of the American Revolution* (New York: Walker & Company, 2002), 84–85.
417. Ibid., 85.
418. New York State Legislature, *Journals of the Provincial Congress*, vol. 2, 140.
419. Leng and Davis, *Staten Island*, vol. 1, 169–70.
420. New York State Legislature, *Journals of the Provincial Congress*, vol. 2, 171.
421. Ibid., 148.
422. Lord Stirling to Samuel Tucker, Esq., President of the Congress of New Jersey, March 2, 1776, *American Archives: Consisting of a Collection of Authentick Records, State Papers, Debates, and Letters and Other Notices of Publick Affairs, the Whole Forming a Documentary History of the Origin and Progress of the North American Colonies; of the Causes and Accomplishment of the American Revolution; and of the Constitution of Government for the United States, to the Final Ratification Thereof; In Six Series*, 4th Series, vol. 5, ed. Peter Force (Washington, D.C.: Congress, 1844), 131–32.
423. Ibid., 132–33.
424. Bayles, *History of Richmond County*, 168.
425. New York State Legislature, *Journals of the Provincial Congress*, vol. 1, 429.
426. Papas, *That Ever Loyal Island*, 55.
427. Leng and Davis, *Staten Island*, vol. 1, 171.
428. Governor Tryon to Lord George Germain, April 13, 1776, in *Documents Relating to the Colonial History of the State of New York*, vol. 13, 676–77.
429. Leng and Davis, *Staten Island*, vol. 1, 171.
430. General Putnam to the President of Congress, April 7, 1776, *American Archives*, 811.
431. Papas, *That Ever Loyal Island*, 56.
432. *The Letter-Book of Captain Alexander McDonald of the Royal Highland Emigrants, 1775–1779* (New York: New York Historical Society, 1882), as quoted in Papas, *That Ever Loyal Island*, 56.

433. Papas, *That Ever Loyal Island*, 57.
434. General John Morin Scott to the New York Provincial Congress, July 5, 1776, in *American Archives*, as quoted in Papas, *That Ever Loyal Island*, 61.
435. Papas, *That Ever Loyal Island*, 64.
436. John Bakeless, *Turncoats, Traitors, and Heores: Espionage in the American Revolution* (New York: Da Capo Press, 1998), 108.
437. Schecter, *Battle for New York*, 101.
438. Papas, *That Ever Loyal Island*, 65.
439. Ibid., 77.
440. Vice Admiral Molyneux Shuldham to Philip Stephens, July 6, 1776, "Disposition of His Majesty's Ships and Vessels in North America under the Command of Vice Admiral Molyneux Shuldham," in *Naval Documents of the American Revolution*, vol. 5, 948.
441. Ibid.
442. Journal of H.M.S. *Rose*, Captain James Wallace, July 2, 1776, in *Naval Documents of the American Revolution*, vol. 5, 989, 895–96.
443. Schecter, *Battle for New York*, 100–1.
444. Journal of Bartholomew James, entry of June 10 to July 4, 1776, in *Naval Documents of the American Revolution*, vol. 5, 920.
445. Major Charles Stuart to His Father, the Earl of Bute, July 9, 1776, in *Naval Documents of the American Revolution*, vol. 5, 989.
446. Journal of Lieutenant Colonel Stephen Kemble, July 5, 1776, in *Naval Documents of the American Revolution*, vol. 5, 937.
447. Captain Ephraim Manning to George Washington, July 3, 1776, in *Naval Documents of the American Revolution*, vol. 5, 894.
448. Journal of Lieutenant Colonel Stephen Kemble, July 5, 1776, in *Naval Documents of the American Revolution*, vol. 5, 937.
449. Brigadier General Nathanael Greene to George Washington, July 5, 1776, in *Naval Documents of the American Revolution*, vol. 5, 935.
450. "Examination of James MacFarlan a Soldier in the 55th Regt Deserted from Staten Island July 4th or 5th 1776," in *Naval Documents of the American Revolution*, vol. 5, 936.
451. Ibid.
452. Ibid.
453. Ibid.
454. Ibid.
455. Ibid.
456. Leng and Davis, *Staten Island*, vol. 1, 171.
457. Papas, *That Ever Loyal Island*, 68–69.

458. Philip Ranlet, "British Recruitment of Americans in New York During the American Revolution," *Military Affairs* 48, no. 1 (January 1984): 26–28.
459. Ibid., 71.
460. Leng and Davis, *Staten Island*, vol. 1, 172–73.
461. Captain Blake, in Charles Anthon, ed., "Anthon's Notes," in *Proceedings of the Staten Island Institute of Arts and Sciences* (Staten Island, NY: Staten Island Institue of Arts and Sciences, 1883), as quoted in Leng and Davis, *Staten Island*, vol. 1, 173.
462. Leng and Davis, *Staten Island*, vol. 1, 173.
463. Anthon, "Anthon's Notes," 160, as quoted in Papas, *That Ever Loyal Island*, 71.
464. Papas, *That Ever Loyal Island*, 71.
465. Ibid., 69–70.
466. Ibid., 70.
467. Major Francis Hutchenson to Major General Francis Haldimand, July 10, 1776, in *Naval Documents of the American Revolution*, vol. 5, 1,011.
468. Journal of Lt. Colonel Stephen Kimble, July 13, 1776, in *Naval Documents of the American Revolution*, vol. 5, 1,063.
469. Brigadier General Hugh Mercer to John Hancock, July 20, 1776, in *Naval Documents of the American Revolution*, vol. 5, 1,158–59.
470. Ibid.
471. Brigadier General Hugh Mercer to George Washington, July 14, 1776, in *Naval Documents of the American Revolution*, vol. 5, 1,077.
472. Journal of Ambrose Serle, July 14, 1776, in *Naval Documents of the American Revolution*, vol. 5, 1,076.
473. Ibid.
474. Burrows and Wallace, *Gotham*, 233.
475. Vice Admiral Richard Lord Howe to George Washington, July 13, 1776, in *Naval Documents of the American Revolution*, vol. 5, 1,062.
476. The spot was marked with a bronze plaque by the Sons of the American Revolution in 1892. However, since that time, a parking lot was built around it, and it's often covered by extra bicycle rack barricades and only noticed when a member of the city council accidentally taps it with a rear bumper. The situation is a source of personal aggravation for the author.
477. Burrows and Wallace, *Gotham*, 232.
478. Morris, *Morris's Memorial*, 207–8.
479. Proclamation by Admiral Howe and General Howe, July 14, 1776, *Naval Documents of the American Revolution*, vol. 5, 1,075–76.
480. Burrows and Wallace, *Gotham*, 234.

481. George Collier, entry of August 12, 1776, "The War in America 1776 Original Manuscript Journal by Admiral Sir George Collier," in *Naval Documents of the American Revolution*, vol. 6, 1,517.
482. Schecter, *Battle for New York*, 123, 126.
483. Vice Admiral Richard Lord Howe to Philip Stephens, August 31, 1776, in *Naval Documents of the American Revolution*, vol. 6, 374.
484. Ibid.
485. Schecter, *Battle for New York*, 131–32.
486. Ibid., 159–61.
487. Ibid., 161–63.
488. Journal of Ambrose Serle, August 30, 1776, in *Naval Documents of the American Revolution*, vol. 6, 362–64.
489. Exchange of Letters Between General Sullivan and Lord Howe, August 30, 1776, in *Naval Documents of the American Revolution*, vol. 6, 364.
490. Ibid.
491. Schecter, *Battle for New York*, 175.
492. John Adams to Abigail Adams, September 6, 1776, in *Naval Documents of the American Revolution*, vol. 6, 726.
493. Founders Online, "Benjamin Franklin to [Lord Howe], September 8, 1776," National Archives, updated February 1, 2018, http://founders.archives.gov/documents/Franklin/01-22-02-0353. [Original source: *The Papers of Benjamin Franklin*, vol. 22, *March 23, 1775, through October 27, 1776*, ed. William B. Willcox (New Haven, CT: Yale University Press, 1982), 591–93.]
494. Benjamin Franklin to William Temple Franklin, September 10, 1776, in *Naval Documents of the American Revolution*, vol. 6, 773.
495. Adams Family Papers: An Electronic Archive, Massachusetts Historical Society, sheet 43 of 53, http://www.masshist.org/digitaladams.
496. Ibid., sheet 44.
497. Ibid.
498. Ibid., sheet 45.
499. Ibid.
500. Founders Online, "Lord Howe's Conference with the Committee of Congress, 11 September 1776," National Archives, updated February 1, 2018, http://founders.archives.gov/documents/Franklin/01-22-02-0358. [Original source: *Papers of Benjamin Franklin*. 598–605.]
501. Journal of Ambrose Serle, September 15, 1776, in *Naval Documents of the American Revolution*, vol. 6, 843.

Chapter 5

502. Papas, *That Ever Loyal Island*, 83.
503. NYPL Map Warper: Layer 869.
504. Bayles, *History of Richmond County*, 248.
505. General Sir William Howe to Lord George Germain, June 7, 1777, in *Naval Documents of the American Revolution*, vol. 9, 11.
506. Vice Admiral Richard Lord Howe to Philip Stephens, June 29, 1777, in *Naval Documents of the American Revolution*, vol. 9, 188.
507. Johann Conrad Döhla, *A Hessian Diary of the American Revolution*, trans. ed. Bruce E. Burgoyne, (Norman: University of Oklahoma Press, 1990), 43–44.
508. Papas, *That Ever Loyal Island*, 81.
509. Ibid., 72–73.
510. Ibid., 73–74.
511. William Stryker, *The New Jersey Volunteers (Loyalists) in the Revolutionary War* (Trenton, NJ: Naar, Day & Naar, 1887), 4–5.
512. Landmarks Preservation Commission, "KREUZER-PELTON HOUSE, 1262 Richmond Terrace, Staten Island. One-Room Original Building Completed in 1722; Addition Completed 1770; Two Story Brick Addition Completed 1836," August 24, 1967, http://s-media.nyc.gov/agencies/lpc/lp/0341.pdf.
513. John R. Cuneo, "The Early Days of the Queen's Rangers: August 1776–February 1777," *Military Affairs* 22, no. 2 (Summer 1958): 65–74.
514. Committee of Safety to General Washington, August 26, 1776, New York State, Dept. of State, in *Calendar of Historical Manuscripts, Relating to the War of the Revolution, in the Office of the Secretary of State, Albany, N.Y* (Albany, NY: Weed, Parsons & Co., 1868), 465.
515. Ibid., 66–69.
516. Ibid., 74.
517. John Graves Simcoe, *Simcoe's Military Journal. A History of the Operations of a Partisan Corps, Called the Queen's Rangers, Commanded by Lieut. Col. J.G. Simcoe, during the War of the American Revolution; Illustrated by Ten Engraved Plans of Actions, &c.* (New York: Artlett & Welford, 1844), 109, 158.
518. Leng and Davis, *Staten Island*, vol. 1, 186.
519. Ibid., vol. 5, 239.
520. *Royal Gazette*, "Queen's Rangers," Advertisement, November 29, 1780.
521. Governor Tryon to Lord George Germain, July 8, 1776, Governor Tryon to Lord George Germain, April 13, 1776, in *Documents Relating to the Colonial History*, vol. 13, 681.

522. Ibid.
523. Leng and Davis, *Staten Island*, vol. 1, 181.
524. Ibid.
525. Bayles, *History of Richmond County*, 204–5.
526. Leng and Davis, *Staten Island*, vol. 1, 182.
527. Bayles, *History of Richmond County*, 205.
528. Leng and Davis, *Staten Island*, vol. 1, 182.
529. Johann von Hinrich, "Description of New York, Long and Staten Islands, in 1776," in *Letters of Brunswick and Hessian Officers During the American Revolution*, trans. William L. Stone (Albany, NY: Joel Munsell's Sons, 1891), 194–95.
530. Döhla, *Hessian Diary*, 37.
531. Major Charles Stuart to His Father, the Earl of Bute, July 9, 1776, in *Naval Documents of the American Revolution*, vol. 5, 989.
532. "Draught of the Watering Place, & Redoubts Constructed to Defend It. 15th July 1776," in *Naval Documents of the American Revolution*, vol. 5, 990. Courtesy of the William L. Clements Library, University of Michigan, Ann Arbor.
533. William T. Davis, "Staten Island Names. Ye Old Names and Nicknames," *Proceedings of the Natural Science Association of Staten Island* 5, no. 5 (March 14, 1896), reprinted in *Proceedings of the Natural Science Association of Staten Island*, vol. 4, ed. Arthur Hollick (New Brighton, NY: Printed for the Association, 1895), 66.
534. NYPL Map Warper: Layer 1035.
535. NYPL Map Warper: Layer 869.
536. Davis, *Conference of Billopp House*, 66.
537. Ibid.
538. NYPL Map Warper: Layer 869.
539. Bayles, *History of Richmond County*, 238.
540. William B. Wilcox, "Too Many Cooks: British Planning before Saratoga," *Journal of British Studies* 2, no. 1 (November 1962): 56–62.
541. John Montresor, *The Montresor Journals*, ed. G.D. Scull (New York: Printed for the Society, 1882), 427.
542. Ibid., 504.
543. Morris, *Morris's Memorial*, 210.
544. Simcoe, *Simcoe's Military Journal*, 120.
545. Morris, *Morris's Memorial*, 209.
546. Major Francis Hutchenson to Major General Frederick Haldimand, July 10, 1776, in *Naval Documents of the American Revolution*, vol. 5, 1,011.

547. Ibid.
548. Joseph Dally, *Woodbridge and Vicinity: The Story of a New Jersey Township* (New Brunswick, NJ: A.E. Gordon, 1873), 242.
549. Leng and Davis, *Staten Island*, vol. 1, 182–83.
550. Ira K. Morris, "Historic Landmarks of Staten Island," in *Ninth Annual Report, 1904, of the American Scenic and Historic Preservation Society* (Albany, NY: Oliver A. Quayle, 1904), 133.
551. Morris, *Morris's Memorial*, 209; NYPL Map Warper: Layer 1035; Automobile Club of America, "A Tour on the Tory Isle," *Club Journal* 3, no. 13 (September 30, 1911): 445–48.
552. Morris, *Morris's Memorial*, 209.
553. Automobile Club of America, "Tour on the Tory Isle," 447–48.
554. John Andre, *Andre's Journal: An Authentic Record of the Movements and Engagements of the British Army in America from June 1777 to November 1778 as Recorded from Day to Day by Major John Andre*, ed. Henry Cabot Lodge (Boston: Bibliophile Society, 1903), 44, 49.
555. Morris, *Morris's Memorial*, 209.
556. Ibid.
557. Charles Clay, "The History of the Staten Island Athletic Club," *Outing* 11, no. 4 (January 1888), 340–51. Morris's description lists the site as the house of the SIAC, which has since been destroyed.
558. Morris, *Morris's Memorial*, 210; NYPL Map Warper: Layer 1035.
559. Sergey Kadinsky, *Hidden Waters of New York City: A History and Guide to 101 Forgotten Lakes* (New York: Countryman Press, 2016), 91.
560. Simcoe, *Simcoe's Military Journal*, 119.
561. Ibid.
562. NYPL Map Warper: Layer 1035.
563. NYPL Map Warper: Layer 869.
564. Davis, *Conference of Billopp House*, 67.
565. Ibid.
566. *Plan of the Redoubts at Richmond on Staten Island, 30th October*, 1779, Library of Congress, https://www.loc.gov/item/gm71000694.
567. Staten Island Antiquarian Society, "Lord Howe Spring," in *History, Story, Legend of the Old King's Highway: Now the Richmond Road* (Staten Island: Staten Island Antiquarian Society, 1916), 25.
568. Reginald Pelham Bolton, "The 'Old Fort,' and Camp-site at Richmond, Staten Island: Explored by the Committee on Field Exploration of the New York Historical Society," *New York Historical Society Quarterly Bulletin* 3, no. 3 (October 1919): 83–88.

569. Ibid., 84–85.
570. Leng and Davis, *Staten Island*, vol. 1, 180–81.
571. Papas, *That Ever Loyal Island*, 66.
572. Schecter, *Battle for New York*, 123.
573. G.J.A. O'Toole, *Honorable Treachery: A History of U.S. Intelligence, Espionage, and Covert Action from the American Revolution to the CIA* (New York: Atlantic Monthly Press, 1991), 29.
574. Bakeless, *Turncoats, Traitors and Heroes*, 166.
575. John F. Schroeder, Benson J. Lossing and Edward C. Towne, *The Life and Times of Washington*, vol. 2 (Albany, NY: M.M. Belcher Publishing, 1903), 981–82.
576. Bakeless, *Turncoats, Traitors and Heroes*, 177–78.
577. Ibid., 178–79.
578. Committee on Revolutionary Pensions, "John L. Mersereau—Heirs of. (To accompany Bill H.R. No. 737.) May 18, 1860," in *Reports of Committees of the House of Representatives, Made during the First Session of the Thirty-Sixth Congress: 1859–'60* (Washington, D.C.: Thomas H. Ford, 1860), 1–2.
579. Bakeless, *Turncoats, Traitors and Heroes*, 181.
580. Bayles, *History of Richmond County*, 240.
581. Papas, *That Ever Loyal Island*, 86.
582. Harry T. Mahoney and Marjorie L. Mahoney, *Gallantry in Action: A Biographic Dictionary of Espionage in the American Revolutionary War* (Lanham, MD: University Press of America, 1999), 126.
583. Bakeless, *Turncoats, Traitors and Heroes*, 179.
584. Ibid., 194–95.
585. Morris, *Morris's Memorial*, 298.
586. Leng and Davis, *Staten Island*, vol. 1, 195.
587. Papas, *That Ever Loyal Island*, 95–96.
588. Raymond Tysen, as quoted in Leng and Davis, *Staten Island*, vol. 1, 195.
589. Papas, *That Ever Loyal Island*, 96.
590. Ibid., 97–98.
591. Raymond M. Tysen, *A Lecture on the History of Staten Island; Delivered before the Tompkinsville Lyceum* (Staten Island, NY: F.L. Hagadorn, 1842), 10.
592. Papas, *That Ever Loyal Island*, 84–85.
593. Ibid., 85–86.
594. Ibid., 86–87.
595. Bayles, *History of Richmond County*, 215; Papas, *That Ever Loyal Island*, 88.

Chapter 6

596. Schecter, *Battle for New York*, 224.
597. John T. Goolrick, *The Life of General Hugh Mercer* (New York: Neale Publishing Company, 1906), 14.
598. Brigadier General Hugh Mercer to George Washington, October 16, 1776, in *Naval Documents of the American Revolution*, vol. 6, 1,292.
599. Bayles, *History of Richmond County*, 183.
600. Brigadier General Hugh Mercer to George Washington, October 16, 1776, in *Naval Documents of the American Revolution*, vol. 6, 1,292–93.
601. Goolrick, *Life of General Hugh Mercer*, 53.
602. Bayles, *History of Richmond County*, 185.
603. Leng and Davis, *Staten Island*, vol. 1, 183.
604. John W. Fortescue, *A History of the British Army* (London: Macmillan, 1899), 212.
605. Döhla, *Hessian Diary*, 37.
606. Ibid.
607. Stephen Popp and Joseph Rosengarten, "Popp's Journal, 1777–1783," *Pennsylvania Magazine of History and Biography* 26, no. 1 (1902): 25–41.
608. Fortescue, *History of the British Army*, 212–13.
609. Andre, *Andre's Journal*, 48.
610. Ibid., 49.
611. Leng and Davis, *Staten Island*, vol. 1, 183.
612. Bayles, *History of Richmond County*, 191.
613. Montresor, *Montresor Journals*, 427.
614. Döhla, *Hessian Diary*, 45.
615. Ibid., 44.
616. Stryker, *New Jersey Volunteers*, 29.
617. Bayles, *History of Richmond County*, 192.
618. Major Lewis Morris's Testimony. G. No. 10, "Major-General John Sullivan. [Charges against him; Proceedings of a Court of Inquiry, including Testimony, Letters and Certificates approving his Conduct in the Staten Island Expedition, and the Battle on the Brandywine, 1777]," New Hampshire Colony, Probate Court, in *Provincial and State Papers*, vol. 17, 178.
619. Stephen Kemble, "The Journals of Lieut-Col Stephen Kemble," in *Collections of the New York Historical Society for the Year 1883, Publication Fund Series* (New York: Printed for the Society, 1883), vii.
620. Bayles, *History of Richmond County*, 192.

621. Reverend Mr. T.F. Armstrong's Testimony, *Provincial and State Papers*, vol. 17, 176.
622. Major Edward Sherbourne's Testimony, *Provincial and State Papers*, vol. 17, 167.
623. Döhla, *Hessian Diary*, 45.
624. Kemble, "Journals of Lieut-Col Stephen Kemble," 127.
625. Döhla, *Hessian Diary*, 45.
626. "[A Scetch [*sic*] of That Part of Statten Island from the Old Star [Ferry] to Deckers Ferry and the Lands Lying to the Westd. Of the Road Leading from Deckers Ferry to the Old Star Made from a View of the Same by Thomas Millidge Major of the 5th Battn. of N: JV]," University of Michigan Library Digital Collections, http://quod.lib.umich.edu/w/wcl1ic/x-1819/wcl001909.
627. Major John Taylor's Complaint, Revolutionary War Rolls, Adjutant-General's Office, vol. 11, 137. As printed in *Provincial and State Papers*, vol. 17, 154.
628. Morris, "Major-General John Sullivan," 226.
629. *New York Gazette and Weekly Mercury*, September 1, 1777.
630. Major John Taylor's Complaint, *Provincial and State Papers*, 154.
631. Andrew Lee, "Extract from Diary of Captain Andrew Lee," *Pennsylvania Magazine of History and Biography* 3 (Philadephia: Publication Fund of the Historical Society of Pennsylvania, 1879), 170.
632. Major Edward Sherbourne's Testimony, *Provincial and State Papers*, 168.
633. Major John Taylor's Complaint, *Provincial and State Papers*, 154.
634. Rev. Mr. T.F. Armstrong's Testimony, *Provincial and State Papers*, vol. 17, 176–77.
635. Morris, *Morris's Memorial*, 227.
636. Major John Taylor's Complaint, Revolutionary War Rolls, Adjutant-General's Office, vol. 11, 137. As printed in *Provincial and State Papers*, vol. 17, 155.
637. Major Taylor's Statement, *Provincial and State Papers*, vol. 17, 162.
638. Major Edward Sherbourne's Testimony, *Provincial and State Papers*, vol. 17, 168.
639. Lee, "Extract from Diary," 171.
640. Ibid., 172.
641. Kemble, "Journals of Lieut-Col Stephen Kemble," 127.
642. Bayles, *History of Richmond County*, 195.
643. Döhla, *Hessian Diary*, 47.
644. Ibid.

645. Ibid., 49.
646. Ibid.
647. Leng and Davis, *Staten Island*, vol. 1, 187.
648. Morris, *Morris's Memorial*, 231–32.
649. Montresor, *Montresor Journals*, 504.
650. *New York Gazette and Weekly Mercury*, July 27, 1778.
651. Montresor, *Montresor Journals*, 505.
652. Ibid., 506.
653. *New-Jersey Gazette*, "Extract of a Letter from Elizabeth-Town, June 6," June 10, 1778.
654. Anthon, *Anthon's Notes*; as quoted in Davis, *Conference of Billopp House*, 133–34.
655. *Royal Gazette*, "New York, June 17," June 17, 1778.
656. Bayles, *History of Richmond County*, 202.
657. *New York Gazette and Weekly Mercury*, "New York, March 22," March 22, 1779.
658. Ibid.
659. "Extracts from the Old County Records, without Special Regard to Dates, *Verbatim et Literatim*," as quoted in Clute, *Annals of Staten Island*, 155.
660. 1820 U.S. Census Westfield, Richmond, New York; Ancestry.com.
661. *New York Gazette and Weekly Mercury*, "New York, March 22," March 22, 1779.
662. William C. McGinnis, *History of St. Peter's Church in Perth Amboy, New Jersey: 1685–1956* (Woodbridge, NJ: Woodbridge Publishing, 1956), 41.
663. Dally, *Woodbridge and Vicinity*, 259–60.
664. *Royal Gazette*, "New York, July 3."
665. Elisha Boudinot to Christopher Billop, November 6, 1779, as quoted in Dally, *Woodbridge and Vicinity*, 260.
666. *Royal Gazette*, "New-York, November 3," November 3, 1779.
667. Ibid.
668. Simcoe, *Simcoe's Military Journal*, 116.
669. Ibid.; *Royal Gazette* "New-York, November 3."
670. Simcoe, *Simcoe's Military Journal*, 277.
671. Ibid., 269.
672. *New-York Gazette*, "Trenton, Janu 10," January 24, 1780.
673. Simcoe, *Simcoe's Military Journal*, 120.
674. James Bailey, "Two Winters of Discontent: A Comparative Look at the Continental Army's Encampments at Valley Forge and Jockey Hollow," in *Pennsylvania's Revolution*, ed. William Pencak (University Park: Pennsylvania State University Press, 2010), 318.

675. Leng and Davis, *Staten Island*, vol. 1, 191. Confirmed by a map: Capt. Reinhard Jacob Martin, "The Attempt Made by the Rebels upon Staten Island January 15th 1780," Sir Henry Clinton Collection, University of Michigan Library Digital Collections, http://quod.lib.umich.edu.
676. Todd W. Braisted, "How George Washington Saved the Life of Abraham Van Buskirk's Son," *Journal of the American Revolution* (September 16, 2014), https://allthingsliberty.com.
677. Joseph Plumb Martin, *The Adventures of a Revolutionary Soldier* (Hallowell, ME: Glazier, Masters & Co., 1830), 124.
678. Martin, "Attempt Made by the Rebels."
679. Edwald G. Schaukirk, "Occupation of New York City by the British," *Pennsylvania Magazine of History and Biography* 10 (1886): 428. Excerpts of Schaukirk's diary include news he heard secondhand, like this story.
680. Bayles, *History of Richmond County*, 200. Both Bayles and Morris quote, but do not name, the author of this letter.
681. Ibid.
682. Simcoe, *Simcoe's Military Journal*, 121–22.
683. Ibid.
684. Ibid., 123.
685. Ibid., 124.
686. Martin, *Adventures of a Revolutionary*, 124.
687. Founders Online, "To George Washington from Major General Stirling, 16 January 1780," National Archives, last modified April 12, 2018, http://founders.archives.gov. Original source: Benjamin L. Huggins, ed., *The Papers of George Washington*, vol. 24, *1 January–9 March 1780* (Charlottesville: University of Virginia Press, 2016), 160–64.
688. Simcoe, *Simcoe's Military Journal*, 128.
689. Ibid., 127.
690. Letter to George Washington from Major General Stirling, January 16, 1780.
691. Ibid.
692. Bailey, "Two Winters of Discontent," 318.
693. Joseph Tuttle, "Washington in Morris-County, New Jersey," *Historical Magazine and Notes and Queries, Concerning the Antiquities, History and Biography of America* 9, no. 6 (June 1871): 377; Leng and Davis, *Staten Island*, vol. 1, 193.
694. Leng and Davis, *Staten Island*, vol. 1, 193.
695. Simcoe, *Simcoe's Military Journal*, 131–32.
696. Ibid., 132–33.
697. Ibid., 133–34.

698. Martin, *Adventures of a Revolutionary*, 126.
699. Ibid., 131.
700. Governor James Robinson to Lord George Germain, July 1, 1780, in *Documents Relating to the Colonial History*, 793.
701. Edwin F. Hatfield, *History of Elizabeth, New Jersey: Including the Early History of Union County* (Elizabeth, NJ: Carlton & Lanahan, 1868), 487.
702. John Hills, surveyor, and William Faden, *Sketch of the Position of the British Forces at Elizabeth Town Point after Their Return from Connecticut Farm, in the Province of East Jersey*, 1784, Norman B. Leventhal Map Center, https://collections.leventhalmap.org.
703. Morris, *Morris's Memorial*, 236.
704. Hills and Faden, "Sketch of the Position."
705. Hatfield, *History of Elizabeth*, 488.
706. Historical Society of Pennsylvania, "Wilhelm, Baron Innhausen and Knyphausen," *Pennsylvania Magazine of History and Biography* 16, no. 2 (July 1892): 239–45.
707. *New-Jersey Journal*, June 14, 1780; New Jersey State Library Digital Collections, http://www.njstatelib.org.
708. Popp and Rosengarten, "Popp's Journal," 34–35.
709. Letter from Governor James Robinson to Lord George Germain, July 1, 1780.
710. Simcoe, *Simcoe's Military Journal*, 143.
711. Bayles, *History of Richmond County*, 147.
712. Popp and Rosengarten, "Popp's Journal," 35.
713. Davis, *Conference of Billopp House*, 146.
714. Ibid., 153.
715. Simcoe, *Simcoe's Military Journal*, 254.
716. *New Jersey Gazette*, "Trenton, August 29," August 29, 1781, as quoted in *Documents Relating to the Revolutionary History of the State of New Jersey*, ed. Austin Scott, vol. 5, *Newspaper Extracts Relating to New Jersey, October 1780–July, 1782* (Trenton, NJ: Staten Gazette Publishing, 1917), 178.
717. Leng and Davis, *Staten Island*, vol. 1, 197.
718. Ernest L. Meyer and J. Schedler, *Map of Elizabeth Town, N.J. at the Time of the Revolutionary War,—1783. Showing That Part of the Free Borough and Town of Elizabeth, Which Is Now the Site of the City of Elizabeth*, 1879, https://www.loc.gov/item/75692375.
719. Leng and Davis, *Staten Island*, vol. 1, 197.
720. Bayles, *History of Richmond County*, 215.
721. *New York Gazette*, "New-York, July 8," July 8, 1782.

722. *Royal American Gazette*, New York, July 23," July 23, 1782.
723. Ibid.
724. Phillip R. Vorhees, "New Jersey's Revolutionary Flotilla-Men in New York's Watermen," *New York Genealogical and Biological Record* 21 (1890): 95.
725. Leng and Davis, *Staten Island*, vol. 1, 196.
726. Clute, *Annals of Staten Island*, 107–8.
727. Leng and Davis, *Staten Island*, vol. 1, 341.
728. Bayles, *History of Richmond County*, 239.
729. Ibid.
730. Milton Klein, "Why Did the British Fail to Win the Hearts and Minds of New Yorkers?" *New York History* 64, no. 4 (October 1983): 357–75.
731. Ibid., 365–66.
732. Papas, *That Ever Loyal Island*, 99.
733. Bayles, *History of Richmond County*, 225–26.
734. Lord Rawdon to the Earl of Huntington, August 5, 1776, as quoted in Papas, *That Ever Loyal Island*, 100.
735. Leng and Davis, *Staten Island*, vol. 1, 198–201.
736. Papas, *That Ever Loyal Island*, 107.
737. Davis, *Conference of Billopp House*, 157.
738. Oscar Zeichner, "The Loyalist Problem in New York after the Revolution," *New York History* 21, no. 3 (July 1940): 284–302.
739. Davis, *Conference of Billopp House*, 169.
740. Leng and Davis, *Staten Island*, vol. 1, 203.
741. Ibid., 198.
742. To Sir Guy Carleton, December 2, 1783, in George Washington, *The Writings of George Washington from the Original Manuscript Sources, 1745–1799*, ed. John C. Fitzpatrick, vol. 27 (Washington, D.C.: Government Printing Office, 1938), 254; Leng and Davis, *Staten Island*, vol. 1, 203; De Vries, "Korte Historiael Ende," 211.
743. *Independent Journal*, "New-York, December 8," December 8, 1783.
744. Clute, *Annals of Staten Island*, 126–27. It is unclear who Clute's eyewitness actually was.

ABOUT THE AUTHOR

Joseph Borelli is a member and minority whip of the New York City Council, representing the South Shore of Staten Island since 2015. He also serves as the chairman of the council's committee on fire and emergency management, which has oversight of the Fire Department of New York and the office of emergency management. Prior to this, he was a member of the New York State Assembly, representing the Sixty-Second District of Staten Island between 2013 and 2015.

Joe is an adjunct professor of political science at the College of Staten Island and was a Lindsay Fellow at the CUNY Institute of State and Local Governance. He is a contributor to the Hill and regularly appears as a commentator on Fox News, Fox Business, CNN, CNNI, HLN, BBC, OAN, AM970 and WABC. He has been published in the *New York Daily News*, *New York Post*, *Washington Times*, *Washington Examiner*, *Staten Island Advance*, *Gotham Gazette* and City & State New York. He serves as a spokesman for the New York State Republican Party.

Joe received a bachelor of arts in history from Marist College and a master of arts in history from the College of Staten Island at the City University of New York. He lives in Annadale with his wife, Rachel; two sons, Joseph Jr. and John; and an overweight English bulldog, Luna.